Preparing Your NVQ Portfolio

A step-by-step guide for candidates at levels 1, 2 and 3

Glenn Clarke

KOGAN PAGE

London • Stirling (USA)

This book is dedicated to my mother

First published in 1997

Kogan Page Limited
120 Pentonville Road
London N1 9JN
and
22883 Quicksilver Drive
Stirling, VA 20166, USA

© Glenn Clarke, 1997

British Library Cataloguing in Publication Data

A CIP record for this book is available from the British Library.

ISBN 0 7494 2465 6

Typeset by JS Typesetting, Wellingborough, Northants.
Printed and bound in Great Britain by
Biddles Ltd, Guildford and King's Lynn

Contents

Contents

Acknowledgements

I would like to thank my wife Pat and my children Emma and Thomas for their encouragement and forbearance while I completed this project during six hectic weeks of March and April.

I would like to thank the 'team' who advised, encouraged and cajoled me: thank you Sue, Judith, Val, Karen, Andrea, Liz and Jayne. Thanks are also due to Ian and Sharon for their technical help and advice and for sorting out a number of minor problems.

Finally, I would like to thank the group of NVQ assessors and candidates that I work with. Without always knowing it they have given freely of their time and ideas and this book could not have been written without them: special thanks to Susan, Liz and Helen.

If I have forgotten anyone it was not intentional. Sorry, but I really have been busy!

Introduction

I have written this book because my work with National Vocational Qualification (NVQ) candidates at levels 1, 2 and 3 has continually demonstrated the need for clear guidance in portfolio preparation. There is currently a lack of such guidance despite the central importance of portfolios to the NVQ process. NVQs are less about academic achievement than they are about practical abilities, but the most practical people are not necessarily the best able to prepare a portfolio, which is an entirely academic exercise. NVQs also put much more responsibility for managing their learning on the shoulders of the individual learner, candidate or trainee and guidance for these people is often thin on the ground. A book such as this is long overdue.

The book is intended to be a practical handbook and will guide NVQ candidates from any occupational area. It sets the scene by describing how NVQs fit into the overall framework of qualifications, how they are structured and how they are assessed. Readers are taken through the first steps of portfolio preparation, guided in their production of essential documentation and shown how to generate and collect the evidence that they will need to successfully complete their portfolios. The book contains portfolio guides throughout the text. These guides highlight the most important considerations in portfolio preparation and they are summarised for easy reference at the end of each chapter.

Probably the most important feature is my attempt to demystify the language of NVQs. NVQ candidates constantly complain to me that they do not understand the stationery they receive as part of their NVQ programmes, nor do they understand the language used in NVQ documentation. I have therefore tried to make this book jargon-free and have written it in plain English. Of course, it is impossible to write a book about NVQs and never use NVQ terminology. I have included a glossary and a list of abbreviations to clearly explain any NVQ jargon used. The book also includes examples of the paperwork that NVQ candidates are expected to complete during their programme. These examples are all drawn from official NVQ documentation and are designed to illustrate the procedures which NVQ candidates are expected to follow.

Anyone launching themselves straight into the NVQ process at level 4 (without having completed an NVQ at level 1, 2 or 3) will also find the book to be of use since they are unlikely to have any experience of portfolio preparation. Students completing GNVQ courses are also required to prepare portfolios and will find much information here about collecting and generating evidence; while this will undoubtedly be of use to them the detailed discussion concerning the organisation and indexing of portfolios is specific to NVQ programmes only.

Finally, the book offers brief guidance for anyone wishing to find out more about NVQs.

Throughout this book I have referred to NVQs, but the discussion equally applies to Scottish Vocational Qualifications (SVQs). In Scotland NVQ levels are generally written as I, II and III rather than 1, 2 or 3; otherwise there is no substantial difference between SVQs and NVQs.

Chapter 1

What are NVQs?

If you have bought this book you probably know what NVQs are. However, a short description is essential if you are going to understand clearly the portfolio building process and means of assessment on which NVQs rest. These processes are very different from other ways of obtaining qualifications, hence the need for a book such as this to explain them. So, how are NVQs different?

THE QUALIFICATIONS FRAMEWORK

Anyone wishing to obtain qualifications under our existing education system is faced with three possible routes: academic, vocational and work-based. The academic route is the one with which most people are familiar. It involves obtaining GCSEs, A-levels and ultimately a degree from university. This education route requires a lengthy period of study followed by the gruelling practice of sitting formal examinations that test how much you know about each subject you have studied.

The vocational route may be less familiar to you and at the moment is undergoing a period of rapid and far-reaching change. Vocational qualifications provide a broad range of knowledge for a number of different occupational areas; these qualifications are mainly grouped within the General National Vocational Qualifications (GNVQ) framework and relate to 14 major occupational areas. Just like academic qualifications they require a period of study, some tests and the production of a number of written assignments or projects. They may also include short periods of work placement and formal examinations. Work-based qualifications or NVQs are very different from these two well-established routes.

NVQs were introduced in 1986 with the intention that they would ultimately replace other job-related courses. The main features of NVQs can be summarised in this ten-point guide.

1. NVQs demonstrate what you can actually do in a work situation and not simply what you know about a subject or an occupation.
2. NVQs develop the skills, knowledge and understanding needed at work and show that you are able to carry out work tasks to agreed national standards consistently and in a range of different circumstances.
3. For the purposes of NVQs it does not matter if your abilities have been gained at work, at college, through experience, by distance or flexible learning methods or even through community work. NVQs simply require you to demonstrate your ability to do a particular job to the standard required by industry.
4. NVQs do not have any entry requirements which you have to meet before you can get started, nor do they have formal written examinations.
5. NVQs are available at five levels, level 1 being the lowest and level 5 the highest.

   Level 1 relates to a range of routine and predictable work activities with many candidates receiving substantial levels of instruction at colleges and other assessment centres.

   Level 2 work activities will be less routine and more complex involving team work, autonomy and individual responsibility. There will be less guidance from, or attendance at, colleges and assessment centres.

   Level 3 work activities will be non-routine, complex tasks with much individual responsibility and some control or guidance of other people. Attendance at assessment centres may be limited to the occasional portfolio workshop or specialised training session.

   Level 4 and 5 work activities will be highly complex technical, professional and managerial functions with considerable autonomy and personal responsibility.

   After discussion with an NVQ assessor and your employer you can enter the NVQ structure at whatever level is appropriate for your existing skills and background. Therefore, you do not have to start at level 1 and work your way up.

6. NVQs are work-based and you do not always need to attend a formal course of study at a college. Candidates at levels 1 and 2 are likely to have limited work experience and their technical knowledge may not be as broad-based as it should be. For these reasons candidates at lower levels may be advised to attend an assessment centre (usually a local further education college) to undertake additional training while completing their NVQs. In particular, candidates at level 1 are likely to find their NVQ programme very similar to a traditional course but with a much greater practical element and the added challenge of preparing a portfolio. But, NVQs are not training programmes or courses, although they may involve some training, and they will certainly require you to register at an assessment centre.

7. NVQs are made up of units which can be taken separately. Because of this you can work towards a full or a partial NVQ at your own pace; you do not have to follow a strict programmed timetable which is outside your control. Unit credits, or certificates, can be built up as slowly or as quickly as you wish.

8. It is possible to transfer units from one NVQ to another and from one assessment centre to another if you change jobs or move house. NVQs are therefore very flexible.

9. If you have, and can prove that you have, the necessary abilities you can be assessed for an NVQ without doing additional training. This is accomplished by producing a portfolio of evidence which is, of course, what this book is about.

10. Finally, NVQs cover thousands of trades, professions and occupations and there is almost certainly one for you.

To sum up the NVQ approach, it is like the driving test. This is a practical assessment of standards which are clearly understood by everyone. How long people may take to reach the level of ability required by the standards is irrelevant; it could be two weeks or two years. It is also immaterial how they were taught or by whom; if you learned from the local driving school or from your wife it does not matter. To pass the test, or assessment, you simply have to show what you can do and what you understand. The same approach is used by NVQ programmes; all that matters is your successful performance in the workplace.

Portfolio Guide: Step 1

Before you can begin thinking about preparing your portfolio you must clearly understand how NVQs differ from traditional examination-based qualifications. If you are not completely sure about this read the ten-point guide to NVQs again. You must immerse yourself in the NVQ philosophy and way of thinking. You can forget examinations.

THE NVQ FRAMEWORK

At the top of the NVQ framework is the National Council for Vocational Qualifications (NCVQ), which is responsible for the quality and organisation of the whole NVQ system. Reporting to the NCVQ are approximately 130 Lead Bodies representing every occupational area and composed of leading experts in their field. The Lead Bodies and NCVQ have devised standards to cover all occupations; these standards specify the tasks that an NVQ candidate has to be able to perform competently, consistently and in a range of circumstances if they are to become qualified.

The standards are subdivided into units, elements, performance criteria and range statements (the terminology may sound strange, but do not worry about it now as it will be fully explained in later chapters). These standards are issued to NVQ candidates who then compile portfolios of evidence (with the help of their assessors) to demonstrate how their abilities at work match those listed in the standards.

When candidates feel that they are able to meet the required standard their portfolio is assessed and if all goes well they are deemed to be competent and are awarded their NVQ certificate. Certificates are not graded like GCSEs or A-levels because they represent an assessment of your ability to do a particular job; you can either do the job in which case a certificate will be issued, or you cannot do the job in which case a certificate will not be issued. But, nothing that you do towards an NVQ is wasted effort: if you fail to obtain your certificate the first time you can provide additional evidence and re-submit your portfolio or you can submit your work for the award of a lower level NVQ.

NVQ candidates do not normally come into direct contact with either the Lead Bodies or the NCVQ. Their involvement in the NVQ process is managed by awarding bodies, assessment centres, verifiers and assessors; each of these groups of people help the candidate to interpret the NVQ standards so that they can prepare a portfolio of evidence which demonstrates their ability or competence to work in a manner which consistently meets or exceeds those standards.

Portfolio Guide: Step 2

Be sure that you are clear about the roles of the NCVQ and the Lead Bodies. Although you do not come into contact with them they have a supervisory role and guarantee the quality of your qualification. They also exist as final authorities in the unlikely event of you being unfairly assessed.

So, how do you 'take' or obtain an NVQ? This question along with the role of awarding bodies, assessment centres, verifiers and assessors is discussed in the next chapter on 'How to take an NVQ'.

SUMMARY

Step 1

Make sure that you understand the differences between NVQs and traditional examination-based qualifications.

Step 2

Ensure that you are clear about the roles of the NCVQ and the Lead Bodies.

Chapter 2

How to take an NVQ

Lead Bodies established by the NCVQ are responsible not only for issuing the national standards for each occupational area, but also for inspecting the schemes of learning and assessment designed by awarding bodies. If these arrangements are found to be acceptable the awarding body is then accredited or authorised to offer that particular NVQ programme to the public. Awarding bodies are often the NVQ candidate's first contact with the NVQ system.

AWARDING BODIES

Awarding bodies have been carefully questioned and inspected by the NCVQ before being validated or accredited. This means that the NCVQ is happy to allow them to interpret the NVQ standards, implement and administer an assessment system and issue successful candidates with their NVQ certificates. There are about 140 awarding bodies and between them they represent every occupational area. Some of them you will have heard of, such as the Royal Society of Arts (RSA) and City and Guilds of London Institute (CGLI), but there are many other more specialised ones such as these:

> British Agricultural and Garden Machinery Association
> Institute of Housing
> Hairdressing Training Board
> National Computer Centre
> Timber Trade Federation
> Worshipful Company of Saddlers.

Because there are so many different awarding bodies the paper-work associated with a particular NVQ and its portfolio building requirements will be different for the same NVQ issued by a different awarding body. Do not let this worry you; the aim of this book is to help you to produce an excellent portfolio which will be acceptable to any awarding body.

If you would like to take an NVQ in a particularly specialised area you will probably have to contact an awarding body yourself (see Further Information, page 114) otherwise your only contact with your awarding body will be on two occasions. First, when you join or enrol on your NVQ programme they will send you a registration slip confirming that you are an NVQ candidate with them. Second, when you have completed your programme they will send you your NVQ certificate. The vast majority of your programme will be conducted by an assessment centre using a number of assessors and verifiers.

Portfolio Guide: Step 3

Familiarise yourself with the different awarding bodies in your occupational area either by speaking to colleagues who are experienced in NVQs or by reading the advice given in Further Information (page 114).

ASSESSMENT CENTRES

In order to obtain an NVQ you will have to register at an assessment centre, or in exceptionally specialised cases direct with an awarding body. An assessment centre is likely to be a college of further education, but it can also be a private training agency or even your workplace. Many large organisations are able to offer their own training schemes and it is increasingly common for them to offer NVQ programmes to their employees.

The assessment centre will require you to enrol as a student or candidate on your chosen programme. They will then contact the awarding body and register you as an NVQ candidate. This is important because this registration will result in you being given a set of the standards that have to be met by your portfolio of evidence.

The assessment centre will probably want to interview you to decide upon your level of ability and ensure that you are on the correct NVQ programme, alternatively they may send you a self-assessment form to complete. This process is often called skills analysis, skills scan or action planning. It is extremely important for two reasons.

First, it will lead to the preparation of an action plan which describes any specific actions that you are required to undertake. These may be simple administrative tasks such as 'provide copies of your existing qualifications' or more complex tasks designed to correct any weaknesses which might affect your chances of gaining an NVQ. Perhaps you will be asked to improve your computer skills, learn more about health and safety at work, or improve a particular skill required in your area of work.

Second, the process of checking your existing skills may reveal that you are exempt from some NVQ requirements because you already have the necessary skills and knowledge. In NVQ jargon you may be able to obtain Accreditation of Prior Learning (APL) which is discussed below.

In order to become an assessment centre an organisation must be approved by the NCVQ; they must therefore have made adequate arrangements to ensure that the quality of their NVQ programmes is acceptable and can be maintained. The organisation's claims will be carefully checked by awarding bodies on behalf of the NCVQ and external verifiers will regularly call in at the assessment centre to make sure that everything is still up to scratch. It is worth noting that, in the unlikely event of you being unfairly assessed, all assessment centres are required by the NCVQ to maintain written appeals procedures and to inform NVQ candidates about them.

Portfolio Guide: Step 4

Find and contact your nearest NVQ assessment centre and see if they can offer you the NVQ that you would like to complete; if they cannot help contact the appropriate awarding body yourself and ask for assistance in finding a suitable assessment centre.

> ## Portfolio Guide: Step 5
>
> Enrol on the NVQ programme that you found.

ACCREDITATION OF PRIOR LEARNING

Explained simply, APL allows you to present evidence of your past work and experience which shows that you already meet the requirements of some of the national standards for your occupation. APL is for anyone who may have acquired skills or knowledge without necessarily receiving formal training or qualifications. The experience that you use must be current and your assessment centre must be satisfied that you can still reach a level of performance today that you might have acquired some time ago.

Furthermore, your past experience must still reflect current practice. For example, a first aid certificate that your acquired 20 years ago will not be acceptable because first aid skills need to be updated regularly. Apart from this condition of currency the assessment centre will have to satisfy themselves that the prior learning for which you are seeking accreditation is relevant to the NVQ programme that you are enrolling on.

The APL process will allow you to see the value of your past experiences and learning by relating them to clearly defined national standards and having them formally assessed. In this way you can gain recognition for the skills, knowledge and experience which you already possess and become aware of areas needing further development. The benefits of APL are of undoubted value to you:

- it enables you to take responsibility for your own career development;
- it allows you to build upon your experience;
- it helps you to develop flexibly and at your own pace;
- it enables you to highlight areas of weakness and take steps to improve your performance;
- it reduces the time and expense needed for you to complete your NVQ;

- it can reduce the workload involved in gaining an NVQ;
- it can avoid the unnecessary duplication of learning.

APL is too complicated a subject to discuss in detail but it is a means by which you can finally gain credit for hard work done without the benefit of formal qualifications. If you already have substantial experience of a job why do you need to enrol on a pre-set course of training? What you need is an assessment system that will identify and credit your existing abilities while highlighting areas of weak ability where top-up training may be required. The team of assessors and verifiers provided by your assessment centre will be willing to discuss APL with you at great length because it can also make their tasks much easier to accomplish.

Portfolio Guide: Step 6

At you initial interview with an NVQ assessor discuss carefully his or her approach to APL. Stress your existing skills and abilities and work out an acceptable APL programme.

ASSESSORS AND VERIFIERS

The assessment centre will have a team of assessors and verifiers who are specialists in your occupational area and an assessor will be appointed to guide you through the NVQ process. The assessor is your ally whose job is:

- to explain the NVQ standards and make sure that you fully understand them;
- to question you about your work and observe you at work so that you can demonstrate your knowledge and understanding;
- to identify weaknesses in your abilities and arrange instruction so that they do not prevent you obtaining an NVQ;
- to help you to prepare your portfolio and organise it correctly for assessment and verification.

As their name suggests, 'assessors' have assessing as their primary function; they assess your performance at work. Assessment is carried out to establish that you can do your job to the required standard, to identify any areas in which you need to improve, and to record your progress. Assessment is carried out on NVQ programmes in three ways: observation, questioning and examining the evidence. This book is about the third method, that of preparing your portfolio of evidence for examination, but your NVQ programme will invariably involve you in the other two forms of assessment.

Observation consists of watching normal everyday work activity and perhaps also observing you, the candidate, in training sessions; if the latter form of observation is used in your case you should be clearly informed beforehand and told what is required of you and what activities you are to perform.

Questioning may sometimes take the form of short simple tests or multiple-choice tests, but it is far more likely to be oral questioning and is aimed at checking the depth of your underpinning knowledge and understanding. Checking your portfolio of evidence is currently the most favoured and extensively used method of assessment and it is therefore the one upon which you should expend most energy, time and commitment.

When the assessor is happy that your portfolio of evidence is ready to be inspected, he or she will sign a statement to that effect and the portfolio will be kept at the assessment centre until it can be verified. After this it will be returned to you.

Verifiers are divided into internal and external verifiers. Internal verifiers are employed by the assessment centre. They will check your portfolio when your assessor feels that it is finished and proves your competence at your job. If everything is satisfactory the internal verifier will countersign the assessor's statement. If there is a problem and you are required to produce extra evidence of your abilities, the verifier will make that decision and advise you accordingly. When your assessor and internal verifier are in agreement they will inform an external verifier and arrange for him or her to visit the assessment centre. Your portfolio will again be taken from you for the purpose of this visit but will be returned afterwards.

The external verifier is an expert in your occupational area and will typically be a prominent civil servant, a businessman, an industrialist or a manager in public service. They are employed directly by the awarding bodies and have no connection with your assessment centre. Their role is:

- to check thoroughly that your assessment centre has done its job efficiently and properly;
- to ensure that your assessor has advised you correctly and rectified any occupational weaknesses that may have existed;
- to ensure that the internal verifier has checked your assessor's decisions and dealt fairly with your case.

Your assessment centre will not call in the external verifier if there are any problems with your work. Therefore, by the time that he or she is called in, your NVQ is in the bag! The final stage in the process is to sit back and wait for your NVQ certificate to arrive.

Portfolio Guide: Step 7

Read the section on assessors and verifiers again until you are perfectly clear about their roles.

1. Assessors are your allies and will guide you through the NVQ process.
2. Internal verifiers will check the assessor's work and your evidence. They will draw attention to any deficiencies.
3. External verifiers will check that assessors and internal verifiers have done their jobs properly and will award you the relevant unit credits.

Of course the whole process rests upon your ability to produce a good portfolio of evidence and that is what the following chapters of this book are about.

SUMMARY

Step 3

Check that there is a suitable awarding body for your occupational area.

Step 4

Contact an assessment centre or enlist the help of the appropriate awarding body to find a centre and see if they can offer the NVQ that you would like to complete.

Step 5

Enrol on an NVQ programme.

Step 6

Check whether or not you can claim APL and exempt yourself from some of the NVQ requirements.

Step 7

Read the section on assessors and verifiers again and be perfectly clear about their roles; they are the key to your success.

Chapter 3

The structure of an NVQ

Once you have found an assessment centre and enrolled on your chosen NVQ programme you will receive a set of standards. They will either be given to you one at a time or you may receive all the standards at once. Taken together they are quite impressive and represent a thick, substantial amount of paper, often written in language that is difficult to understand and which is littered with jargon. They can easily be off-putting to candidates and cause them to become discouraged. This is therefore a good point at which to dismantle the standards, to take them apart, show how they work and demystify them.

STANDARDS

Lead Bodies are responsible for defining the standards at each level, from 1 to 5, for each occupation. Awarding bodies are then accredited or licensed to offer NVQs based on these national standards. The standards are written specifications that detail how certain tasks are to be done and how certain functions are to be performed. When a candidate is able to consistently perform the required task in the manner laid down by a standard and can demonstrate that they have the required knowledge they are deemed to be competent.

Awarding bodies work differently from each other and the standards you receive from them may differ slightly from the ideal model which is made up of these three parts:

1. introductory material which explains how to use the standards;
2. the standards themselves;

3. blank forms for you to chart your progress and organise your portfolio.

The forms will be difficult to understand and we will ignore them for the moment; we will look at portfolio indexing (which is really what the forms are for) in some detail later.

Portfolio Guide: Step 8

If blank forms are included with your standards remove them and keep them safe; you will need to use them as master copies later on.

Read the introduction to your standards carefully. Read and read again anything about performance criteria, range statements and evidence requirements because your under standing of these three things is vital to preparing a successful portfolio.

Read the standards themselves and begin to formulate your own plans for meeting them: relate the standards to your everyday work activities. Are you engaged in anything to which you can pay particular attention in order to generate documentary evidence for your portfolio?

Because there are 140 awarding bodies each dealing with a number of different occupational areas, standards for the same task issued by different awarding bodies could be laid out differently from each other. If you come into contact with other NVQ candidates working with awarding bodies different from your own you may become aware of these minor differences. Do not worry about this; the only standards that you are concerned with are those for your own NVQ. And in any case all awarding bodies have been checked by the appropriate Lead Body and their own individual arrange-ments have been approved. Whatever NVQ standards are used in your case you will immediately notice that they are subdivided into units and again into elements.

UNITS

Standards are presented in small manageable parts known as units and each unit of your NVQ can be obtained and accredited separately. However, each NVQ specifies that a certain number or combination of units must be achieved before you can be granted a full NVQ certificate. You will need to look carefully at the units for your NVQ before deciding which combination you would like to complete. Units are of three types: compulsory, optional and additional. Compulsory and optional units are included in all NVQ standards but additional units are less common.

Compulsory units must be completed if you are to obtain your certificate. They are sometimes called mandatory units or core units and are designed to check your knowledge of the fundamental principles upon which your occupation rests. You may also notice that at levels 1 and 2 the compulsory units of some standards act as a check upon your basic skills in maths, English and computers. Check your standards to see which units you must complete; if you are in any doubt your assessor will be able to explain them to you.

Optional units bring some element of choice into the standards allowing you to complete units in which you have a particular interest or in which you are especially able and can demonstrate a good deal of expertise. When making a choice of optional units you are well advised to read all of the units first and choose those which relate to each other as closely as possible. By doing this you can reduce the overall amount of evidence that you have to produce for your portfolio because your evidence may serve to illustrate more than one unit.

If you choose units that are very different from each other you will be faced with producing individual items of evidence for each of them and this can be a long process. Check your standards very carefully to see how many and which combination of optional units you must complete. Again, seek the advice of your assessor when making this choice; he or she will be able to help you to devise the best and most efficient strategy.

Additional units are included in some NVQs in order to provide further career options and to allow candidates to obtain specialised experience in areas that may not normally occur in their workplace. Additional units also allow you to follow up your own interests and develop useful additional skills. They can also serve as useful bridges between NVQ levels which allow you to finish one NVQ level with your feet firmly on the bottom rung of the ladder for the next level. Candidates usually choose to complete additional units for precisely these reasons.

I must repeat that the standards for your NVQ will specify that you complete a certain combination of units and you must meet this requirement. Candidates at level 2 will typically be required to complete three compulsory units and three optional units; while candidates at level 3 can expect to complete four compulsory units and five optional units. Units are the smallest part of an NVQ for which you can gain accreditation but they themselves are subdivided into elements.

Portfolio Guide: Step 9

Discuss the units for your NVQ with your assessor. Make sure that you know which units are compulsory and which are optional. After careful thought and discussion choose optional units which:

1. are related to specific occupational tasks that you are engaged in at the moment, because you can then take particular care to generate and collect evidence
2. are related to each other in some way in order to minimise your NVQ portfolio workload and therefore keep your portfolio to manageable proportions. In other words consider taking closely related clusters of units such as all the IT units or all the customer care units.

ELEMENTS

Each element of an NVQ is made up of the following components:

- the unit and element titles
- performance criteria
- range statements.

The element may also include further information such as the following:

- essential knowledge requirements
- essential understanding requirements
- evidence requirements.

The unit and element titles are self-explanatory, they simply state the task or function that has to be performed. They may also include unique numbers or codes which identify them in your NVQ; for example the National Examinations Board for Agriculture, Horticulture and Allied Industries offers an NVQ level 1 in Amenity Horticulture. This includes five units each divided into a number of elements; here are the titles, elements and numbers for unit 001:

Unit 001	Assist in Establishing Ornamental Plantings and Turf
Element 001.01	Assist with preparing land for planting and sowing
Element 001.02	Assist with planting ornamental plants
Element 001.03	Establish turf by broadcasting seed
Element 001.04	Establish turf by laying turves.

Each element has to be fully completed before credit can be awarded for the unit as a whole.

Performance criteria for each element outline exactly what has to be done by the candidates to establish their competence and they may be used as a checklist when the candidates are observed at work or questioned about their work. For example element 001.04 'establish turf by laying turves' requires candidates to be able to meet the following performance criteria:

- handle and stack turf correctly
- prepare the site
- check turves for damage
- lay turves in the correct manner
- protect turves from pests
- maintain tools and equipment throughout
- adhere to health and safety arrangements throughout.

Performance criteria are clear statements which define an acceptable level of performance: they focus upon only the essential aspects of a task and therefore provide a basis for clear and unbiased assessment.

The range statements are included to allow the candidate to demonstrate their performance under a range of circumstances such as different physical locations, using a variety of equipment, or in different work contexts. For example in the Amenity Horticulture NVQ already mentioned, (a) can candidates lay turf in wet rainy conditions as well as on fine, sunny days? and (b) can they lay turf on a sloping site as well as on a flat one?

Essential knowledge, or underpinning knowledge and understanding, are said to be 'embedded' in the performance criteria but assessors will want to satisfy themselves that candidates are aware of why a task is undertaken in a particular way. This section of the element therefore highlights subjects about which candidates can expect to be questioned. Underpinning knowledge and under standing represent the basic knowledge needed to perform tasks specified in the standards. They are not usually assessed formally in examinations although you may be given short assignments to complete and informal tests may be set from time to time. It is far more likely that you will be questioned in a chatty and informal manner.

Be on your guard when questioning takes place because there is a 'hidden agenda' in the standards. Lead Bodies want to be satisfied not only that you can perform to the required standard and demonstrate relevant knowledge and understanding, they also want to be satisfied that you have the appropriate personal qualities. This is a very vague area and much of it is of a subjective nature:

- Do you relate well to other people?
- Are you concerned about the quality of your work?
- Are you self-confident and assured?
- Do you make an effort to improve your performance?
- Are you appropriately dressed for your occupation?

The only way that an assessor can make a favourable judgement about these things is by reflecting upon what happened when they questioned you, not just by focusing on your answers to the questions and whether they were right or wrong.

The final part of the element, the evidence requirements, explain exactly what evidence the assessors and verifiers will expect to see in your portfolio and is therefore an extremely valuable aid when you come to organise your portfolio, which is the next step.

Portfolio Guide: Step 10

Look very carefully at the elements in your compulsory and optional units. Be clear in your own mind that you can and will achieve them; remember you will be guided at every step of the way by your assessor and this book. Check that you fully understand how the different parts of the elements interact with each other, particularly the performance criteria, the range statements and the evidence indicators. These three are the vital connecting threads that run throughout your portfolio and throughout the whole of the NVQ process.

Portfolio Guide: Step 11

Make sure that you fully understand the structure of an NVQ:

An NVQ title is represented by a set of standards which are divided into a number of units, each of which is subdivided into elements, which contain performance criteria, range statements and evidence requirements that have to be met by your portfolio of evidence. You will also have to demonstrate that your underpinning knowledge and understanding is adequate and that your personal competence is acceptable.

SUMMARY

Step 8

Keep blank NVQ forms safely and make photocopies for use. Read your standards, especially the performance criteria and range statements.

Relate the standards to your work activities and begin to think of ways in which you can collect evidence about them.

Step 9

Make sure that you understand the mixture of compulsory and optional units, and try to choose units that relate to each other.

Step 10

Examine the elements of your compulsory and optional units. If you do not understand them see your assessor and seek clarification.

Step 11

Ensure that you understand the structure of your NVQ.

Chapter 4

Portfolios and evidence

In order to complete your NVQ successfully you must gather together evidence of your work to show that you are able to:

- do
- understand
- achieve

the performance criteria and range statements for each element, within each unit of your chosen NVQ. Because NVQs do not depend upon examinations you need to produce a portfolio, or collection of evidence, that supports your claim for accreditation by clearly demonstrating what you can do, what you understand and what you can achieve.

WHAT IS A PORTFOLIO?

The idea of producing a portfolio may be quite new to you, but portfolios have been used in many areas of work and are fairly commonplace in creative occupations. Budding artists, photographers and designers, for example, will almost certainly have a portfolio containing the best of their work, and fashion models will find that their agency produces a professional photographic portfolio with which to lure prospective clients. But, less glamorous tradesmen also find a portfolio to be of use. The cabinet maker might keep a photographic record of fitted kitchens that he has installed and the landscape gardener will almost certainly be able to provide photographs and plans of her best work. Some portfolios such as those used by soft furnishing and curtain makers could even include examples of fabric, patterns from which to chose and finished samples of tie-backs, piping, etc to show the quality of work. NVQ portfolios are very similar to all of these but they have to be produced and structured in a particular manner if they are to be acceptable to assessors and verifiers.

An NVQ portfolio fulfils three functions:

1. It is a collection of your work and evidence about your work.
2. It supports your claim in seeking accreditation by supplementing your practical activities and providing the major means by which assessors and verifiers will be able to assess your performance.
3. It shows the variety of your experience and the knowledge that you have gained.

Portfolio Guide: Step 12

Read again the functions of an NVQ portfolio and begin to formulate in your mind ideas for collecting evidence which demonstrates your knowledge and experience.

Put very simply, an NVQ portfolio records evidence about your work and how it relates to the performance criteria and range statements specified in the standards. The evidence may relate to recent work or it may be a product of your previous experience. This is important because both your current and past experiences, and your current and past learning, have value and can work together towards gaining you accreditation. This raises the question, 'What is evidence?'

EVIDENCE

Evidence is anything of sufficient quality to be presented in your portfolio as proof of your competence to undertake a specific task to the required standard. Each element of an NVQ includes performance criteria and range statements for which you must produce evidence; they may also contain evidence indicators which will simplify your task. Evidence therefore is the key to successfully completing an NVQ: it is information which confirms that a predetermined standard of performance has been reached consistently and in a variety of circumstances. There are a number of requirements for acceptable evidence. It should be:

1. *Valid:* evidence should be relevant to the performance criteria and range statements. Do not use it simply to 'pad out' your portfolio because this will make the assessor's and verifier's tasks more difficult.

2. *Authentic:* evidence should be genuine; have it witnessed or authenticated as appropriate and use examples of evidence that support each other.

3. *Reliable:* evidence should be capable of being checked or verified and should be presented in a manner which is consistent and cross-referenced in order to aid the assessor's and verifier's understanding.

4. *Sufficient:* evidence should be presented concisely; it should be clear, brief and to the point. Quantity is not a substitute for clear, simple quality.

5. *Current:* evidence should be up-to-date if possible, but if you acquired a skill some time ago, and if that skill is still current and relevant, you still possess the skill and may submit evidence relating to it.

6. *Non-confidential:* if you use evidence which involves information about other people you must respect their confidentiality by removing their names, addresses and other personal information. Likewise if your evidence contains information which has commercial value, includes trade secrets or involves matters of national security you must respect confidentiality and obtain clearance from the relevant authority to use such evidence. Remember that assessors and verifiers do not choose to be burdened with such delicate information, so use it sparingly.

7. *Transferable:* evidence should be capable of being applied in circumstances additional to those in which it was assessed. This is the purpose of range statements in the standards: they give you the opportunity to demonstrate your abilities in a range of circumstances.

Portfolio Guide: Step 13

Try to remember the requirements for acceptable NVQ evidence and match each example of *your* evidence to this list.

Does your evidence meet as many of the requirements as possible?

DIRECT AND INDIRECT EVIDENCE

You may hear assessors and verifiers talking about evidence in different terms; in particular they may discuss the two major types of evidence, indirect and direct. Indirect evidence is provided by other people and testifies to your performance or abilities. It usually takes the form of a testimonial or witnessed statement. We will consider this type of evidence in more detail later. Direct evidence is produced as a direct result of your personal performance at work and takes one of two forms:

1. *Performance evidence* is gathered as a result of your personal actions. Examples of performance evidence are samples of your work, notes of observations, the results of simulations, etc.
2. *Supplementary evidence* supports performance evidence by demonstrating underpinning knowledge and understanding. It usually takes the form of questioning and off-the-job testing.

The evidence that I shall be advising you to collect falls into both of these categories so you do not need to think about them any further; you will be collecting indirect evidence and your portfolio will include performance and supplementary evidence by the time that you have finished.

STARTING YOUR PORTFOLIO

Your portfolio is a collection of evidence and the first thing you need to do is to find somewhere to store your evidence until it is ready to be organised and included in your portfolio. You need a place to keep everything. This might be:

(a)   your desk drawer
(b)   the shelf in your locker
(c)   a cardboard box under your worktable
(d)   a box file
(e)   your pigeon hole.

The place that you choose to keep everything can be at work or at home; it does not really matter, although most people find it more convenient to keep things in their workplace. What does matter is that it should be safe.

Everyone who might come into contact with your collection of evidence (particularly colleagues at work) should know that it is important, valuable and irreplaceable and must not throw it away during the spring clean.

Portfolio Guide: Step 14

Label your work folder clearly with your name and the title of your NVQ.
Keep it safe and securely locked away if possible.

Whatever place you chose to keep your evidence get into the habit of putting into it everything that could possibly be of use. Be methodical about this. Keep copies of everything because you will not know until much later exactly which vital pieces of evidence might be missing.

Exactly what can be used as evidence is discussed in some detail throughout Chapters 6 and 7; for the moment simply get into the habit of keeping anything that demonstrates your ability at work. As you put possible pieces of evidence away for future use write the date on them and keep a simple evidence log book with a brief description of each item of evidence. Next to this description note down the circumstances under which the evidence was created and record your actions along with the reasons for taking them.

Any cheap notebook is adequate for your log and as it is confidential need only make sense to you. Do try to develop the habit of keeping an evidence log because later on in your NVQ programme you will have to describe how your evidence was produced and a logbook will make this task much easier.

You will need a portfolio to organise your collection of evidence. Here is the basic shopping list for a 'portfolio starter kit':

- ring binder
- dividers
- hole punch
- diary or calendar
- glue stick
- scissors
- clear plastic wallets
- plain white paper
- plain coloured paper
- coloured pens
- coloured labels
- plain white labels
- notebook
- pencil.

You might find that you need other things from time to time, but this basic list is sufficient to get you started. It is also helpful if you have access to a photocopier. If one is not available at work you should find out where you can use a machine and become familiar with its operation. All libraries should have a photocopier and many stationery shops and newsagents also offer copying facilities. Do not worry about copyright because you will only be copying:

- your own work
- NVQ forms and stationery
- documents generated as part of your job.

Finally, access to a personal computer and word-processing package is also useful. Your NVQ will almost certainly require you to show some familiarity with computers, but using them to produce smart documentation, cover sheets, memos, letters and the like will help to ensure that your portfolio is of top quality.

Portfolio Guide: Step 15

1. Obtain all the stationery that you will need.
2. Arrange to have access to a photocopier.
3. Arrange to have access to a word-processor and begin learning to use it if you are not already proficient.

Every good portfolio begins with a management section or an introductory section which is not specifically related to the NVQ standards. This section of your portfolio should contain the following documents which you can begin to collect together at any time:

- a cover
- a contents list
- your job description
- job appraisals (or annual staff reports generated at work, sometimes referred to as performance reviews)
- your CV
- photocopies of the structure of your NVQ (ie, the unit standards which your portfolio claims to demonstrate)
- an evidence index
- an introduction or personal statement
- an organisational profile
- an organisational chart.

Portfolio Guide: Step 16

Begin collecting together your:

- job description
- CV
- staff reviews
- photocopy of the overall structure of your NVQ – which you can find in your standards.

Try to obtain an organisational chart and an organisational profile or information about your organisation that will help you to write a simple profile or description.

Chapter 5 will guide you through producing a cover, CV, organisational chart and organisational profile. The remaining documents will be fully explained in later chapters so you should not worry about them at this stage.

SUMMARY

Step 12

Make sure that you fully understand the functions of an NVQ portfolio.

Step 13

Read the section about acceptable evidence again and begin collecting material which meets the requirements discussed.

Step 14

Find somewhere to keep your evidence safely and use it.

Step 15

- Obtain the stationery that you are going to need.
- Arrange to have access to a photocopier.
- Arrange access to a word-processor and begin learning to use it if you are not already proficient.

Step 16

Obtain copies of as many of the following documents as you can:

- your job description
- CV
- the structure of your NVQ
- an organisational profile
- an organisational chart (for the organisation you work for)
- your annual staff reports or performance reviews.

Chapter 5

Starting a portfolio

If you have followed the steps given in Chapter 4 you can begin your portfolio immediately by producing information for the introductory section of your folder, ie documents that do not directly relate to NVQ standards and for which you do not need the guidance of an assessor or verifier. The best place to start is, of course, at the beginning with a cover.

YOUR PORTFOLIO COVER

Your first real task is to produce a cover sheet to go at the front of your portfolio folder or ring binder. You might also find it useful to fix a copy of the cover on the outside of your binder so that it is easily identifiable by work colleagues and by assessors and verifiers during their assessment visits. The cover should be as simple as possible but must contain:

- the name of the organisation you work for
- the title and level of your NVQ
- your name
- the dates covered by your portfolio (since it is not yet completed the starting date will be sufficient, the finishing date can be added later)
- the name of the awarding body for your NVQ.

A sample cover that you could customise for your own use is shown on the next page.

Flixton General Hospital

Advice, Guidance, Counselling and Psychotherapy
Services Support

NVQ 2

Portfolio of Evidence

PATRICIA C CLARKE

January–December 1997

Awarding Body   **Royal Society of Arts**

Figure 5.1   *A sample portfolio cover; you may customise this for your
own use*

Portfolio Guide: Step 17

Produce a cover for your portfolio. Even if it is handwritten, do it now to clearly identify your valuable collection of evidence.

CVs

When you have produced a cover you can begin work on your curriculum vitae (CV) or personal statement. 'Curriculum vitae' is a Latin term, meaning a summary of your life, experiences and qualifications. Such a document is vital for anyone in today's competitive job market and it is therefore worth spending time on this task and producing a high-quality, impressive document.

A CV is necessary in your NVQ portfolio because it tells your assessors and verifiers something about your experience and skills which might not be apparent from the rest of your evidence. It is your chance to tell people how interesting and accomplished you are; it charts your achievements over the years and shows how hard you have worked; it gives a personality or human touch to an otherwise impersonal collection of paperwork and reminds assessors that they are dealing with an individual, a real person. This simple fact is often lost or submerged in the mountains of paper produced by NVQs.

Producing a CV is also a valuable exercise in personal development because listing your experiences and qualifications will highlight any gaps or weaknesses that you have. It is important that you are aware of any shortcomings of this nature since you can take account of them when you prepare your action plans and aim to do something during the course of your NVQ programme which will improve your performance, your effectiveness and your employment prospects.

If you do not have a current CV you need a rough framework in which you can organise your personal details and other relevant information. You can do this quite simply by taking nine sheets of blank paper and writing on each of them one of the following headings:

- personal details
- education
- staff development (training provided by your employer)
- employment
- professional activities
- community activities
- personal activities
- records of achievement
- abilities and strengths.

When you have done that look at the sheets and decide when you must spend some time collecting together information to complete them.

Portfolio Guide: Step 18

Prepare rough sheets upon which to organise your CV.

Decide upon a time when you can complete the sheets by following the instructions given in the next section of this book.

WRITING YOUR CV

The sheet headed 'personal details' should contain the following essential information:

- your name
- your address
- your telephone number (and fax number and/or e-mail address if you have them).

Optional information which you may also include in your personal details would be your date of birth, your marital status and dependants. Whether you include this information or not is entirely up to you. Some people prefer not to divulge things that can have no effect upon their 'employability', others feel that they have nothing to hide and therefore include everything, even their religion which is not always foremost in an employer's mind.

It is fairly obvious what information should be included on the sheet headed 'education'. List schools, colleges and universities attended along with the dates and any qualifications achieved. If you have qualifications make the most of them here; if you don't have qualifications do not despair. Include the fact that you are enrolled at whatever assessment centre to complete your NVQ level 3 in Hairdressing after which you intend to progress to level 4 or whatever your own NVQ is. Make the most of what you have.

The sheet headed 'staff development' should be used to detail any training that you might have received at work. Remember that NVQs are all about work and what you can do; they are not about education and what you know. Consequently any training that you have received at work is worthy of a mention, particularly health and safety training, because it is so prevalent in NVQs from computing to maintenance of overhead power lines and from child care to mortuary practice. Include the title of the training or development programme and the dates that it took place along with the result of any assessment carried out.

The 'employment sheet' is fairly straightforward. For each job that you have had record the dates of your employment; your employer's name, business and address; your job title; a brief list of duties and responsibilities. Start with your current or most recent employment and work backwards. If there are significant gaps in your employment history that will not be explained elsewhere in your CV include a brief statement to clarify the situation. (Perhaps you left work to raise a family, care for a sick relative or were made redundant.) You may feel that your employment history is too sketchy or that there is not enough of it but it is perfectly acceptable to include part-time or fixed-contract work and any periods of self-employment can quite legitimately be included.

If you are a member of any professional bodies or institutes record the relevant information on the sheet headed 'professional activities'. You might simply state the fact that you are a member or you might give a detailed description of the activities you are engaged in along with information about the grade of your membership (student, associate, member, fellow, etc) and any awards that you might have been granted or special projects that you might be involved in. Any voluntary or community work and any fundraising activities that you are involved in now, or have been involved in at some point in the past, should be entered on the 'community activities' sheet along with relevant dates and a brief description of the activities.

Portfolio Guide: Step 19

Collect together as much rough information as you can about your:

- education
- staff development
- employment
- professional and community activities
- hobbies and interests.

Complete your rough CV sheets.

'Personal activities' relate simply to hobbies or interests and this sheet can be used to bring a little life and personality into your CV. This is where you can show some individuality and remind your readers that you are a unique individual. Include whatever you think is appropriate, but if you have interests which directly relate to your occupation it will pay you dividends to explain them here in some detail.

I suggested that you include a sheet headed 'Record of achievement'. Recent school leavers will immediately know what I am talking about and be able to provide this information with ease, since pupils now leave school with a full record of their experience, examinations, work placements and so on. This is often abbreviated to RoA and could well be a mystery to older more mature NVQ candidates. If this is so in your case, use the sheet to record any other significant aspects of your experiences and skills that are not covered elsewhere.

The idea of having a section headed 'abilities and strengths' in your CV is relatively new and you can include it or not as you choose. It is really an opportunity to stress personal qualities that you feel are not adequately covered elsewhere. It is an opportunity to sell yourself by describing how well you communicate, how you relate to other team members, how you are disciplined and self-motivated in your work. If you are happy with this 'hard sell' approach, it will make a useful addition to your CV. If you are worried about it and cannot think of anything to write, exclude it completely and produce the traditional CV with which most people are more familiar.

When you have completed your rough sheets use them to produce your finished CV by organising the information in the standard format shown in Figure 5.2.

Aim to keep your finished CV to just two sides of A4 paper and word-process the document since this is the most flexible option and allows you to add new information with ease (including your newly gained NVQs, for example). Whether you include a list of references on your CV is up to you. References may be either personal character references or formal work-based ones; personally I have a third sheet for my own CV which lists previous employers and named individuals to whom I was responsible along with their telephone numbers. I include this sheet or not depending upon the individual circumstances in which I am using my CV.

Portfolio Guide: Step 20

Use your rough CV sheets and the standard CV layout given here to produce your CV on a word-processor.

ORGANISATIONAL PROFILES

The organisational profile or description is a necessary addition to your portfolio for two reasons. First, it tells the assessors and verifiers something about the organisation that you work for; remember he or she might never have heard of your organisation before and may know nothing about its activities. Second, the profile shows that you know something about the organisation that you work for. This is not as silly as it sounds; it is extremely important to show the assessors and verifiers that you know the aims and objectives of your employer, the size of the organisation of which you are part, and any particular strengths or plans that your employer has. Quite simply, it is professional to be able to demonstrate that you are aware of what is going on around you.

An organisational profile might sound complicated but it is simple to produce and needs to be on only one side of A4 paper. Start the profile by heading your sheet with the organisation's name and the department or section that you work for, and follow this with a brief (just one or two paragraphs) description of the organisation. You can usually find useful information without too

Curriculum Vitae

Personal Details

Name
Address
Telephone number
Date of birth

Education

Date   *School/College*   *Qualifications*

Training

Training completed at work

Employment

Date   *Name and address of employer*

Job title and responsibilities

Professional Activities

Membership of associations with dates and grade of membership

Personal Interests

Voluntary/community work
Hobbies and leisure activities

Abilities and Strengths

References

Figure 5.2 *Standard layout of a CV*

much difficulty; company reports or publicity, college prospectuses, council handbooks, reports and publicity or the council's A to Z of services and many other similar sources of information will all provide you with the facts you need. You can simply copy the information out if it is appropriate or adapt it to suit your needs. An especially useful source of information would be the pack of data sent to job applicants and any induction information given to new employees, so an early port of call in your search should be the personnel department.

If your organisation has a mission statement or charter it is useful to include the most relevant parts of these documents in your profile. You also need to include some statistical information which gives assessors and verifiers a picture of the size of the organisation and the scale of its activities. This information can be drawn from numerous sources since all organisations collect statistical data as an aid to planning and developing their services. If you have any difficulty in obtaining this information, perhaps because it is commercially sensitive, ask your supervisor at work for help and explain why you need it.

Finally, your organisational profile should include information about the size of the department that you work for and a general concluding remark that highlights some particular strength or specific interest of your employer. This needs to be, perhaps, one or two sentences and should be easy enough to prepare simply by looking at your own day-to-day activities.

Portfolio Guide: Step 21

Collect information about the organisation you work for:

- name
- size
- history
- aims and objectives
- unique features
- strengths
- location
- business
- plans for the future
- awards and commendations.

Produce an organisational profile on one side of A4 paper.

When you have completed your organisational profile it can be added to your portfolio. Remember that if several of you are completing NVQs at the same workplace the task of preparing a profile can be shared and it is always possible that a previous candidate, or a candidate more advanced than you, has already prepared an acceptable profile which you can use. This is not 'cheating' because you are not claiming any specific competencies on the basis of your organisation's profile; its purpose is simply to let assessors and verifiers orient themselves and introduce them to your organisation.

Similarly, the final document that you need in the introduction to your portfolio (an organisational structure) aims to familiarise assessors and verifiers with the structure of the organisation you work for and with your individual level of responsibility within that structure.

ORGANISATIONAL STRUCTURES

The extent and detail of the structure that you should include in your portfolio varies tremendously and it is therefore difficult to give hard and fast rules. Generally speaking you should include just enough information to make it clear where you fit into the organisation and how the organisation's structure affects your individual role. Candidates at level 2 therefore will find that a chart relating to their immediate colleagues, supervisor and manager is perfectly adequate for portfolio purposes. If you work for a large supermarket chain, for example, a chart showing the people who work at your local store is adequate; you do not need to include the whole regional organisation. In the example given in Figure 5.3, the candidate is submitting an organisational structure for an NVQ at level 2 and needs to include only the detail shown.

Notice that the candidate has highlighted herself on the chart so that the assessor or verifier can quickly pinpoint her position in the organisation. A candidate working towards a level 3 NVQ would find it important to show assessors and verifiers how their role relates to that of others within the organisation and would therefore produce a more detailed and extensive structure.

You do not need to include people's names if you prefer not to, simply using their job titles is quite sufficient. Additionally, your

---

The Garden Centre
Urmston

Manager
Mr S Ainsworth

Sales Supervisor	**Head Gardener**
❊ Emma ❊	Robert
Sales Assistants	**Assistant Gardeners**
Kimberley	Catherine
Roxana	Terry
Lee	

Weekend Help
Christopher

Figure 5.3 *Simple organisational structure*

chart or structure does not have to be professionally produced like those shown in company reports with lots of complicated boxes and lines of responsibility; hand-drawn or typed examples are perfectly acceptable as is the simple word-processed example shown here. If an organisational chart already exists or has been prepared by other NVQ candidates feel free to make use of it in this context and save yourself some work, because the chart is only for purposes of information; it does not claim that you meet any of the performance criteria or range statements in your NVQ.

If you decide not to include people's names on the chart it may be worth considering adding to your portfolio a list of people referred to in your evidence. The list should be arranged alphabetically and include their job title or responsibilities. This 'cast of characters' is not compulsory but if you feel that it will help assessors and verifiers to understand your evidence you should try to include it.

> ## Portfolio Guide: Step 22
>
> Collect information about the structure of your organisation and your place in the structure.
> Use this information to produce a diagram of the organisational structure on one side of A4 paper.

Producing organisational profiles and structures may seem to be an unnecessary chore to you and you are probably wondering why I am burdening you with these tasks. Apart from the reasons that I have already given there is another vital reason for undertaking this work. When you come to index your completed portfolio you will be required to write several 'unit context sheets' or 'evidence summary sheets'. Do not worry about them at the moment, they are easily and quickly dealt with, but getting into the habit of writing generally about your organisation and coming to terms with its structure will benefit you tremendously when the time comes to write these sheets. Believe me, the effort will be worthwhile but you will not appreciate this until later on in your portfolio.

FIRST STEPS

By now I hope that you are surrounded with paperwork and stationery so let us take the first steps in organising it. Put all of your clear plastic wallets into the ring binder and insert your cover sheet in the first one, also fix a copy of the cover on the outside of your file. Then insert your CV, job description, organisational profile and organisational chart. You now need a brief overview of the unit and element structure for your NVQ and you should find a suitable one, which you can photocopy, in your standards. On the overview of your NVQ, block out with a thick felt-tipped pen all of the optional or additional units and elements that you do not intend to complete. This is a purely psychological step which allows you to concentrate on the list of units and elements that you are doing. Include the list in your folder. Leave about half a dozen empty plastic wallets and insert the first divider in your ring binder to separate the introductory material from your collection of evidence which is to follow. You will be pleased to know that the background section of your portfolio is now complete; it even contains space for action plans, monitoring documents and assessment schemes as you obtain them during your NVQ programme.

Your next task is to organise the rest of your ring binder in such a way that it is ready for you to file in your collection of evidence which will expand rapidly in the coming months. To do this you need a divider and probably half a dozen clear plastic wallets for each element in each unit of your NVQ. Candidates for NVQs at level 2 are required to complete approximately six units each of four or five elements and will therefore need 30 dividers and at least a hundred plastic wallets. Candidates for NVQs at level 3 will be required to complete approximately nine units and will therefore need more dividers and plastic wallets than this.

For the moment I would advise you to invest in just one pack of a hundred plastic wallets and add more when you have gained experience in selecting good quality evidence and have a better idea of the final 'shape' of your portfolio. Experience shows that portfolios rarely exceed one large lever-arch ring binder in size. (Much bigger than this and you run the risk of alienating by boredom your assessors and verifiers.)

Portfolio Guide: Step 23

Fix a cover sheet to the outside of your binder and place a second copy in the first of your plastic wallets.
  Add the following documents to your binder:

- CV
- job description
- organisational profile
- organisational chart
- overview of the units and elements for your NVQ.

Add to your binder the dividers and remaining plastic wallets.

The remainder of your portfolio now exists as a simple framework of dividers and plastic wallets. Basically, you have a filing system which contains a number of documents but which is 90 per cent empty. The next stage is obviously to start filling up your filing system with evidence.

SUMMARY

Step 17

Produce a cover for your portfolio.

Step 18

Prepare rough sheets for your CV.

Step 19

Collect information and complete the rough CV sheets.

Step 20

Produce a good quality CV.

Step 21

Produce an organisational profile.

Step 22

Produce an organisational chart.

Step 23

Begin assembling your portfolio.

Chapter 6

Collecting written evidence

I have said a great deal about evidence in previous chapters but I have always referred to it in NVQ 'speak' or jargon. I have spoken repeatedly about collecting evidence to prove that you can meet performance criteria and range statements, and to prove in assessment situations that you are capable and efficient in your job. I have also described how to set up and organise a folder ready to receive your evidence but it is still 90 per cent empty. Now is the time to look at evidence more closely, to demystify the terminology and speak in plain language.

The evidence that you will be collecting is sometimes referred to as historical evidence and results directly from activities that you have undertaken in the past. Perhaps the easiest way to think of evidence is in legal terms. Whatever is submitted in court, be it a blood-stained knife or a fingerprint on a glass, is presented because it proves something; that 'this is the blood of Mr X', that 'Mrs Y touched this glass'. NVQ evidence is really no different from these examples; this page from an appointment book shows that Mrs A can efficiently organise her team of hairdressers, and this conference itinerary proves that Mr B can communicate effectively with numbers of conference delegates and organise their time effectively. NVQ evidence may not be as exciting as criminal evidence but the underlying principles are exactly the same.

It is unlikely that a criminal will be convicted on the strength of a single piece of evidence, indeed the whole purpose of a trial and all of the investigative effort that goes into it is to collect together a mass of evidence that proves guilt, or innocence. It is the collection of evidence, the ways that different items of evidence support each other, and the pages of supporting testimony from witnesses that ultimately result in a conviction. Likewise with NVQ evidence; one example of an appointment book or one conference itinerary does not prove 'guilt', or competence, over a period of time or in a range of different circumstances. Therefore, each individual item of evidence has to be supported with numerous other items that back up its claims; a single piece of evidence cannot stand on its own.

When you collect your evidence you have to collect items which relate to each other, where each individual item backs up, supports and proves the claims made by other individual items. It is this complex web of interrelated evidence that will establish your 'guilt'; it will prove that you are 'guilty' of doing your job to the required standard time after time and in the widest range of circumstances imaginable.

Portfolio Guide: Step 24

Evidence should be proof: only include in your portfolio evidence which proves your ability. Do not include useless 'padding'.

Evidence should be supported, therefore try to collect examples of evidence that mesh together, that support and prove each other.

If you are going to do this and establish your 'guilt' beyond any shadow of a doubt you have to put evidence as a whole on to the witness stand and find out why and how it becomes evidence.

In all of the portfolios that I have seen the vast majority of evidence is paper-based or written. Even so, evidence can be divided into nine categories, which I will examine in detail in this and the next chapter. You must read these two chapters carefully; if you do not immediately spot evidence which relates specifically to your job then re-read the following pages because they summarise all evidence. The categories of evidence are:

1. General written evidence and correspondence
2. Publicity and advertising
3. Statistical information
4. Information derived from meetings and appointments
5. Graphical information

6. Audio-visual information
7. Computer-generated information
8. Artefacts and products
9. NVQ stationery and forms.

The first four categories are covered in this chapter and the remaining five are discussed in Chapter 7.

Portfolio Guide: Step 25

Try to remember these nine categories of evidence, all of which can be submitted in your portfolio, and begin to collect together whichever of them is appropriate to your NVQ.

---

1. GENERAL WRITTEN EVIDENCE

You have already gathered together some evidence in this broad category and have included it in your portfolio: your CV, job description, job or performance appraisals and the organisational profile and organisational chart that you should have prepared. Copies of your existing qualifications also fall into this broad category and can be included in the introductory section of your portfolio.

At the other end of the spectrum, simple work diaries that demonstrate how you organise your time effectively can also constitute valuable evidence. This illustrates a fundamental lesson: anything that highlights your ability to do your job is potential evidence; a humble work diary can be as valuable as a GCSE certificate.

If you use a work diary it becomes evidence simply by requesting a weekly meeting with your supervisors and asking them to initial it. If this is not possible (perhaps because you are self-employed) ask your NVQ assessor to undertake this duty when you have your regular review meetings. What you are doing is authenticating your evidence by having an independent third party witness it.

Portfolio Guide: Step 26

Anything which proves your ability to do your job is evidence and may be included in your portfolio.

The issue of authenticity of evidence was raised earlier, in Chapter 4, and you should keep it firmly in mind when you collect documents for your portfolio. If your work involves you in producing word-processed documents, develop the habit of including your initials and the date on every piece of work that you print out. Do this by choosing a small-sized typeface and adding your NVQ 'logo' or 'trademark' to one of the bottom corners of the document. Figure 6.1 shows a simple telephone message form designed and produced by an NVQ candidate. Notice that it includes her NVQ 'logo' in the bottom right-hand corner.

Telephone Message

For: _____ From: _____

Message:

_____

_____

_____

_____

❏ telephoned ❏ ring back ❏ will ring back ❏ urgent

taken by: _____ time: _____ date: _____

Ver 3 Jayne Jan '97

Figure 6.1 *Telephone message form with NVQ candidate's 'logo' in the bottom right-hand corner*

You may already have generated a variety of forms, record sheets, memos and leaflets in your work and now realise that they can easily become valuable NVQ evidence. This paperwork is easy enough to include: simply go back to your documents and update them by adding your 'logo' and the version of the document (perhaps it has been revised several times) as shown in the above example. Whenever you are involved in the design, specification or production of a document keep all notes relating to the project and include them in your portfolio along with the finished piece of work. If several people are involved in producing a particular piece of work they should all include their initials (especially if they are fellow NVQ candidates) and all of them can include the work in their portfolios.

Handwritten material is also acceptable as evidence so do not think that evidence may only be presented as smart word-processed documents. Notes of telephone conversations, specifications or details discussed with customers, completed requisitions or order forms and job sheets are just a few examples that spring to mind. If you are in any doubt about establishing the authenticity of a piece of work, have it initialed by a third party or your NVQ assessor, as already described. Alternatively, you might find it useful to produce a blank form which testifies to the authenticity of your work and which can be completed and signed by supervisors, managers, work colleagues, clients or NVQ assessors.

The value of having a ready-made form is that the people you call upon to act as witnesses may not be familiar with NVQs and therefore produce statements which, although they may be very flattering to you, will be so general as to make them worthless as evidence. A pre-printed form can state clearly which NVQ you are completing and exactly which performance criteria and range statements you would like your witnesses to comment upon. An example of a witnessed statement which you might like to adapt to suit your own needs is given in Figure 6.2.

If for some reason you decide not to use forms you can ask witnesses to write what is known as a letter of validation which describes your performance. In order for it to be acceptable as evidence the letter should take the following format:

1. Have it written on the organisation's official headed paper if possible.

2. Clearly state your name and position or job title.
3. List the title of your NVQ and the performance criteria or range statements being claimed.
4. Describe the circumstances in which your competence was demonstrated.
5. Have the letter signed and dated.
6. Include the position or job title of the witness.

Work which has been published in your name as a report or technical document, papers in journals, books and so on do not require authentication; they are automatically evidence and authenticated by virtue of being published. Likewise with documents that mention you by name and that have been widely circulated in your workplace, staff rotas, minutes of meetings that you have attended and many other similar documents. Of course documents and publications are only of value in your portfolio insofar as they relate to the specific performance criteria being claimed.

Correspondence is a rich source of documentary evidence for portfolios and includes memos and letters that are from you to other people, that are addressed to you, or that you have typed or word-processed on behalf of others (in which case, you need to have them authenticated or present them in your portfolio along with the memo requesting you to do the work).

Many of the NVQs based upon clerical activities, and a surprising number of the others, require you to have some familiarity with the transmission and receipt of faxes. If this is so in your case, feel free to include faxes in your portfolio. If you do not normally send or receive faxes, you should consider taking an opportunity to do so and include in your portfolio evidence which, apart from the merits of its contents, also demonstrates your familiarity with modern business equipment and practices.

Testimonials or references from satisfied customers, previous employers and clients that you have helped can also be included under the heading of general written evidence. There is an important lesson for all of us here because we are all guilty of not saying 'thank you' or complimenting others on the quality of their work, consequently such evidence might be thin on the ground. You can, however, force the issue quite simply and generate such evidence; whenever you are asked to complete a particular task at work and would like to include it as evidence in your portfolio, do the task efficiently and follow it up with a brief memo saying

Statement

Candidate: _____

NVQ: _____ Level: _____

I am claiming competence for: _____
Unit: _____
Element: _____
Performance Criteria: _____

(Please make a brief statement that comments upon my ability in working for this unit and element of my NVQ.)

Statement: _____

_____

_____

_____

_____

I have read and understand the relevant performance criteria and range statements for this unit and element.

Witness: _____

Signature: _____ Name: _____

Date: _____

Ver 2 Andrea Feb '97

Figure 6.2 *Sample form for witness statements*

that you have done what was requested. This then gives you the opportunity to explain specific decisions that you took (thus demonstrating underpinning knowledge and understanding) and an opportunity to suggest improvements or new ways of doing things in the future. Furthermore, such memos often result in brief thank you notes, which is exactly what you need for your portfolio.

If you wish, you can of course enlist the aid of your supervisor or manager by getting them involved in your NVQ work, explaining to them how it will benefit the organisation, and asking them for occasional memos that comment upon your performance and effectiveness. If such notes are not complementary or are over-critical of you do not worry, you can omit them from your portfolio.

On my frequent assessment visits to NVQ candidates it is quite common to hear managers and supervisors saying that they know Karen or Liz is doing an NVQ because in the past they simply got on with the job, whereas now they not only seem to be extremely keen but they also put everything in writing forcing them to write back. So, this technique is tried and tested and generally works quite well.

Portfolio Guide: Step 27

You can generate useful evidence whenever you wish by writing memos or letters to your supervisor, manager, work colleagues and outside organisations.

Use this simple but effective tool as often as you need it.

---

2. PUBLICITY AND ADVERTISING

Materials related to publicity and advertising can be a useful source of evidence if you are involved in the specification, design, production or distribution of such documents. Simply including a leaflet in your portfolio with no explanation of your role in its creation is of no use. You must set such materials firmly in context and show why they demonstrate your competence. This can be difficult to do and is almost impossible to achieve retrospectively with materials prepared some time previously.

The best course of action is to switch your mind into NVQ mode as soon as you become engaged in publicity and advertising materials. Therefore keep notes and minutes of any meetings where such materials are discussed and where work roles are allocated. Keep notes relating to the specification or design of the poster, leaflet or advertisement along with reasons that led to the decisions taken and the rejection of alternatives. Keep copies of all rough sketches, layouts, colour schemes, discussions of computer packages to be used, typefaces, font sizes and illustrations. Obtain originals of the completed works and present them in your portfolio with all of the supporting evidence that you have collected. Remember that your portfolio is intended not only to demonstrate competence but competence over a period of time.

Portfolio Guide: Step 28

It is important to demonstrate your abilities over a range of time. Therefore, keep notes of all preliminary discussions, meetings, decisions and the reasons they were taken, plans, rough drafts and finished 'products' for your portfolio. In this way you can show the development of a product, document or idea from its original inception through to its final form.

If you contribute to staff newsletters or are mentioned in them, keep copies. If your workplace is mentioned in the local press, perhaps a hairdressing salon raising money for Comic Relief, keep a newspaper cutting. If your workplace features on television or radio, keep a tape, it might become valuable evidence. (See the section on audio-visual evidence in Chapter 7 for more information.) You will only know whether something is or is not evidence when you gain experience in reading and interpreting the performance criteria and range statements of your NVQ standards. If a press cutting or a tape of a radio advertising jingle in some way shows you meeting a specific performance criteria or range statement it is evidence. Use it.

3. STATISTICAL INFORMATION

I can almost hear you groaning at the mere mention of statistical information but, because all organisations collect statistics for monitoring and planning purposes they represent a rewarding source of evidence. As statistics are so widely used it is difficult to choose specific examples that you might include in your portfolio but most statistics revolve around cash handling and financial matters, production or efficiency targets and user or customer surveys.

If you are involved in financial services of any sort it will not be difficult for you to collect together examples of budget forecasts, accounting spreadsheets, annual accounts and a wealth of similar information that is an everyday part of your job. Samples of any of them which show you meeting performance criteria and range statements are evidence and can be used in your portfolio.

Candidates in many areas of work that are not specifically financial may feel that their opportunities to present this kind of evidence are limited. This is not necessarily the case since your assessor can arrange for you to take part in simulations (activities designed to mimic or imitate the real world) the results of which can be included in your portfolio.

Many people who would not count their work as financial are required to handle cash even if it is only to ensure the smooth running of the tea fund or collecting for the Christmas outing and these activities can all usefully generate evidence of the required nature. Anything that demonstrates your abilities in arithmetic or more complex maths and book-keeping is acceptable evidence and makes a pleasant change for the assessors and verifiers who otherwise read endless reams of letters, memos and reports.

Production targets obviously relate to the factory floor and include the complex calculations involved in deciding how many of a particular product can be manufactured in a week using a three shift system with 18 machines one of which is sure to break down. If this rings a bell with you, include it as evidence. But if it sounds totally alien, think again. If you order the delivery of petrol or diesel for a fleet of vans and lorries how do you arrive at your final figures? If you order stocks of hair conditioner for a hair-dressing salon how do you calculate your stock level? If you are sowing 300 square metres of grass how do you work out how much seed you require and how much seed do you keep in stock given that it might spoil if kept beyond a certain use-by date? I could think of more examples but what you need to do is look at your particular occupation and see what target setting and other calculations you are involved in and whether any of that work become evidence in your portfolio.

If you genuinely are not engaged in any activities like these but would like to use some statistical evidence to demonstrate your abilities in maths, you can generate the evidence easily enough by asking to become involved in appropriate areas of work on a one-off basis specifically for your NVQ, or you can conduct a customer or user survey. This is an ideal opportunity to design a questionnaire or form and distribute it. The results from completed sheets can then be logged and you can set to work analysing them and developing useful new ideas or staffing timetables for your workplace depending upon the questions you have asked.

Portfolio Guide: Step 29

If your work does not involve you in statistical or financial matters and you need such evidence to meet specific performance criteria consider undertaking customer or user surveys.

---

4. MEETINGS

Next time you attend a meeting do so with a new lease of life, be eager and enthusiastic because it is a guaranteed source of useful evidence. The particular value of being at a meeting is that you are in at the start of a project; as soon as a new project or idea is voiced you will be initially involved and then have a perfect opportunity to show how you can contribute to a work-based activity as it develops over a period of time – one of the essential requirements of an NVQ.

When you attend meetings keep careful notes of what is said and any tasks that you accept responsibility for. Keep the agenda and keep the minutes when they arrive; indeed you cannot do better than volunteering to keep the minutes since this allows you to demonstrate your ability to take notes, write them up, word-process and distribute them, have them formally accepted as a true record at successive meetings, and they prove that you attended the meeting as well. What excellent value.

Meetings do not have to be large important gatherings, indeed it is frequently the case that the larger the meeting the less work it gets through. Any meeting can be useful for NVQ purposes: one-to-one meetings with sales representatives to order fresh stocks or one-to-one meetings with customers to discuss their requirements are just as valid as regular team meetings and large formal board meetings. The golden rule is to keep notes, which can be authenticated, and to try your best to make appropriate contributions so that you warrant a mention in the minutes.

Portfolio Guide: Step 30

Meetings are a valuable source of evidence because they provide agendas, notes and minutes.

Small meetings are just as valuable as large formal ones.

Examine your day-to-day work; is there any scope in your contact and meetings with customers and users for you to generate evidence?

Closely connected with meetings are any occasions which require you to receive visitors or to organise the activities of others. Consequently, simple appointment books or more complex conference itineraries are valid evidence. So too are activity plans devised by nursery nurses to keep the play group happy or story-telling hours organised by the library assistant to attract younger readers to the library. Do not think that meetings must necessarily be protracted or long-winded to generate evidence; the briefest person-to-person encounter (if observed by an assessor or witnessed by a colleague) can yield vital evidence not obtainable in other ways. A hairdresser or waiter taking special care to ensure that a client who uses a wheelchair is comfortably accommodated in the salon or restaurant is providing valuable material to meet customer service and equal opportunities criteria.

The different forms of written evidence described here form the backbone of all NVQ portfolios and the ideas and suggestions given here should enable candidates in any occupational area to successfully generate evidence which clearly demonstrates their abilities to do their jobs and meet NVQ criteria. However, evidence can take a number of other forms and all candidates should be aware of the possibilities of using graphics, audio-visual information, computer generated evidence and artefacts and products in their portfolios. These other forms of evidence are discussed in the next chapter which should be read by all candidates including those who feel that they can prepare their portfolios using written evidence alone.

SUMMARY

Step 24

All evidence should prove something and items of evidence should support each other.

Step 25

There are nine categories of evidence; be familiar with all of them and collect whatever is appropriate for your portfolio.

Step 26

Anything that proves your ability is evidence.

Step 27

Write memos, letters and reports to prompt responses and generate evidence for your portfolio.

Step 28

Take care to keep related items of evidence which clearly illustrate the development of a project over a period of time.

Step 29

To generate statistical information consider undertaking a customer or user survey.

Step 30

All meetings are useful sources of evidence. Attend meetings whenever possible and keep notes, agendas and minutes for your portfolio.

Chapter 7

Collecting other forms of evidence

5. GRAPHICS

Graphics in one form or another are applicable to every occupation, so do not be put off by the phrase and dismiss it as something 'arty' in which you are not interested and which never involves you. What follows hardly mentions 'art' at all and your occupation almost certainly makes use of graphics.

Graphics really means presenting information in a form which is not just written, so the portfolio guide boxes in this book can be considered as graphics. At the other end of the spectrum, paintings and drawings represent information that is presented in an exclusively pictorial form, they also are graphics. NVQ portfolios generally contain graphics from one or more of the following categories: charts, technical drawings, maps, sketches, patterns and designs.

Charts may be as simple and commonplace as timetables and year planners which organise your work activities. They may also be more complex diagrams, like that of the structure of an NVQ or flowcharts which explain a complex process or computer program pictorially. We can even include here the design of forms produced to organise workplace information and activities. If your work requires you to produce charts, put your initials on them, have them authenticated and add them to your stock of evidence.

Technical drawings are perhaps more complex and you probably feel that they are unlikely to affect hairdressers, tree fellers or customer care candidates, for example. But technical drawings do not have to be engineering blueprints or architect's plans; almost anything that portrays visually information that could not be given in writing can qualify. A hairdresser's sketch showing a new trainee how to complete a particular razor cut; the arboriculturalist's quick drawing of a tree's major branches and those which need to be removed; the office supervisor's drawing showing the placement of new word-processors, modem, switchboard and fax machine; all of these qualify as 'technical' drawings and, if you have them, should be included in your portfolio. If you are involved in the production of technical drawings at any stage, I repeat: add your name, authenticate them, include them in your portfolio.

You may think that maps do not affect your occupation but they can be included in an amazing variety of portfolios: maps showing the location of the hairdresser's salon, road maps showing where to find the trees that are to be felled, and maps showing the layout of the store and its new customer care service point are just some of the endless possibilities. One example of a map that nearly all NVQ candidates could usefully include in their portfolios to meet health and safety at work criteria is a plan of their workplace which clearly shows the location of fire exits, fire alarm points and fire extinguishers.

With sketches we are moving more into the realms of pure artwork but it is surprising how many NVQ candidates can use sketches as a source of evidence. If we take the three NVQ candidates used as examples above: hairdressers can sketch a new style, arboriculturists can sketch ideal tree shapes, shop workers can sketch the new service point layout, etc. Use your imagination and if sketches seem to be an appropriate form of evidence, use them. Please do not think that you must include artistic evidence for your NVQ portfolio to be accepted, it is simply a possibility. If you cannot draw then do not attempt it; include in your portfolio only what you can do. The portfolio aims to get you credit for what you can do and can do well, its purpose is not to draw attention to what you cannot do.

Designs do not necessarily mean completed artwork although if you are completing an NVQ in fashion and have superb designs you should use them. For NVQ purposes designs can mean many things from rough layouts and suggested contents of forms or Internet Web pages, to designs for printing layouts and even designs of products and packaging that are to be manufactured. They may be rough and even scribbled on scrap paper but they are important because they show the developmental process of a product, a new record form, a magazine layout, etc in action and this is a vital requirement of NVQ evidence; it should be produced over a period of time. So, keep your rough notes, plans and drawings safe, they are proof.

Patterns are also useful evidence although they are so specialised that they will not be of interest to the majority of NVQ candidates. I am thinking of patterns such as those produced by toolmakers in engineering, but also the paper patterns produced by dressmakers and tailors. One could even include stencils, templates or cardboard patterns designed for young children to draw round (to make posters) or to cut round (eg, to make glove puppets).

Portfolio Guide: Step 31

Examine the different types of graphical information discussed here and see which of them are used in your workplace and in your occupation.

Do they demonstrate your abilities? Do they show you meeting performance criteria?

If they do, they are evidence and can be included in your portfolio.

My aim here has not been to list every single possible item of evidence but to suggest to you the rich variety of material that can usefully be submitted in a portfolio. If it applies to you then collect examples of your work, authenticate them and include them.

6. AUDIO-VISUAL EVIDENCE

Audio-visual evidence takes the form of photographs, audio tapes and video tapes. It is interesting because it can fulfil one of two functions: it can be evidence in its own right by proving that you have devised, produced and scripted a 'talk in' radio programme, or it can be evidence of something else by recording on videotape, for example, the fact that you conducted a guided tour of a stately home, a museum or a library. If you work in any of the media-related industries then there is not a lot that I can tell you about the possibilities of audio-visual evidence and where I have spoken previously about written evidence you can legitimately include photography, sound recordings and moving image recordings in your NVQ portfolio. These media will be assessed and verified just as if they were written documents by experts in the particular field of your occupation.

However, for those of you who do not work in these industries I need to describe the different features of these forms of evidence and give you clear guidance on how to use them. Photographs need no special arrangements in order to make them effective items of evidence in a portfolio other than an explanation of what the photograph is intended to portray and a statement of the performance criteria and range statements that you are claiming.

Photographs are particularly useful when the 'product' of your occupation may not be available for assessment. For example, a hairdresser cannot keep her clients waiting until the assessor arrives to inspect the hairstyle. What you can do of course is (with the client's permission) take a photograph and a short written statement expressing the client's delight with the new style.

Likewise, a landscape gardener might not be able to guarantee an assessment visit to a particularly challenging site before and after she gets to work. But she can easily take before and after photographs as well as photographs showing the development of the site as flowers and shrubs bloom and become well-established.

This approach to recording your work produces excellent and unusual evidence and with a little imagination can be employed in a wide variety of occupations: photographs of the storeroom, office or reception area before and after reorganisation, for example. Photographic evidence is also the only way of presenting to an assessor something which will not survive until his next scheduled visit: a temporary display for example or a particularly spectacular cake. A final use of photographs is as a way of presenting products or artefacts that cannot be included in a portfolio simply because they are too big and cumbersome.

An especially useful feature of some modern cameras is known as 'title printing' and results in photographs that have the date and time that they were taken printed discreetly in the corner or on the back of the print. This is particularly valuable for NVQ candidates because the photograph is automatically given an element of authenticity and because large collections of photographs can easily be sorted into date order. Some candidates may have access to digital cameras which can record their pictures directly into a computer. If you are fortunate enough to have access to such sophisticated equipment, use it but read the comments below about computer-generated evidence and how to use it with special attention.

If you feel that photographic evidence will enhance your portfolio or solve some of the problems that you would otherwise be unable to deal with, by all means use photographs, but do not include them just to make your folder look pretty. Like all evidence, photographs have to be relevant and they have to demonstrate your claim to meet specific performance criteria and range statements.

Portfolio Guide: Step 32

Read the notes on photographic evidence again and decide how photographs may be used to enhance the evidence presented in your portfolio.

Remember to seek permission from clients before photographing them and refer to the notes on confidentiality of evidence before taking photographs of sites or equipment that may be government controlled or of particular commercial value (see page 26).

The use of audiotapes and videotapes as evidence is also acceptable in NVQ portfolios but their use is more problematical than photographs. Like photographs these media have the advantage that they make accessible to an assessor events or products that are temporary or will not survive until an assessment visit can be arranged. But, unlike photographs they convey nothing themselves: they have to be played and listened to or viewed.

This presents you with two problems. First, your portfolio will not stand alone on its own merits: it needs the support of a video and television or a cassette player. If you use evidence of this nature, it is up to you to make sure that when an assessor or verifier visits your workplace or assessment centre the necessary equipment will be available and working.

Second, you run the risk of boring the assessor who may have to sit through half an hour of videotape in order to reach the ten seconds where you claim to meet a particular performance criterion. There are two ways of dealing with this problem. Have the tape edited or re-recorded so that you present as evidence only the few vital moments where you claim a performance criterion. Having this work done can be expensive and might be beyond your means unless you know an enthusiastic amateur.

The second solution is to clearly label the tape and state that between clock settings 327 and 348, for example, you will demonstrate your competence at a particular task and therefore claim performance criterion seven or whatever. This is by far the most practical approach if you use audio-visual evidence and the one I urge you to adopt. The label should state clearly:

(a)   your name
(b)   the title of your NVQ
(c)   the date of recording
(d)   the circumstances under which the recording was made
(e)   clock settings to use
(f)   performance criteria and range statements claimed.

Of course, there is no guarantee that it really is you in the video or that you are actually speaking on the audiotape; remember your evidence has to be authentic and capable of being verified. The way to achieve this with audio-visual evidence is to attach a signed witness statement to the effect that the person shown or heard on the tape really is you. Alternatively, where you submit a lot of audio-visual evidence, you might wish to include in your portfolio a photograph of yourself which has been authenticated by your assessor or a brief audio recording of your voice also authenticated by your assessor.

Portfolio Guide: Step 33

If you decide to include in your portfolio evidence on audiotape or videotape you must do the following two things:

1.   Clearly label your tapes as described.
2.   Keep duplicate copies of the recordings in case disaster strikes and the originals go missing.

By all means use audio-visual evidence, but be sure that it is relevant and not a time-wasting portfolio 'frill' that achieves nothing extra. And, most important of all, make absolutely sure that it is clearly labelled and that duplicate copies exist.

7. COMPUTER-GENERATED EVIDENCE

Computer-generated evidence is if anything more problematical than audio-visual evidence and suffers from the same fundamental weakness in that it needs a machine to access it. This is compounded by the fact that computer-generated evidence also needs a particular operating system and software package to make it work. If you submit this sort of evidence it is up to you to ensure that suitable equipment and software are available and running properly when assessment visits take place – and such visits will occur several times during your NVQ programme. Having said that, you should still include computer-generated evidence if it supports your claim to meet a particular performance criteria; if it is relevant include it in your portfolio. What exactly can you include and how?

The safest course of action is to include in your portfolio examples of what the 'electronic product' does and an explanation of how you developed the 'product'. If you wish to include a computer program for example (perhaps one that works out the estimated cost of wear and tear on a heavy goods vehicle per 1000 miles of operation), include in your portfolio one or two of the statements produced by your program. Support this with the printed program listings and any documentation that shows the program under development and being tested. A copy of the disk containing the program can also be included should the assessor or verifier wish to try the program for themselves.

Finally, a signed witness statement attesting to your authorship should also be included; this is vital because a floppy disk on its own proves nothing. The same basic limitation applies to all computer-generated evidence, ie there is no intrinsic proof in the floppy disk itself, or in the e-mail message, or in the Internet Web page. None of them contains information that can be easily verified and establish you as the undisputed author of the material rightly and justly claiming to meet performance criteria.

If you submit evidence held on magnetic media you must label it clearly with:

(a)   your name
(b)   your NVQ title
(c)   the word-processing package, spreadsheet or programming language used
(d)   the operating system used
(e)   which machines it is compatible with
(f)   a description of its uses
(g)   a description of the circumstances under which it was produced.

Furthermore this information must be supported with witness statements to the effect that this really is your work.

Portfolio Guide: Step 34

If you submit electronic evidence in your portfolio you must do three things:

1. Clearly label it as described.
2. Include a hard copy of the 'product' of your work: listings, spreadsheets, calculations, etc.
3. Keep back-up copies of the disks.

---

8. ARTEFACTS AND PRODUCTS

Artefacts and products refer to things that you have made, physical objects that have been produced as a result of your work. They may have been produced by high-tech automated processes (cars, washing machines, television sets) or hand made in a craft-based 'cottage industry' (pottery, tailored clothing, fine book bindings, traditional wooden toys). Whatever the product is, it is unlikely that you will be able to present it in a ring binder full of plastic wallets and it is unwise to commit yourself to the chore of hauling round samples of your work every time that an assessment visit is scheduled.

If a product is small and portable enough it may be possible to include actual examples in a box file or some other form of packaging. For example, I have seen a portfolio that included a box file containing two hand-made wigs! If you need to resort to adding a box file or some other sort of container to your portfolio (and there is absolutely no reason why you should not), follow the golden rules of identifying your work. Clearly label additional folders, boxes or containers with your name, the title of your NVQ and a brief description of the contents so that your assessor is not as shocked as I was when I found the wigs.

Just as computer-generated evidence, or videotapes, or photographs prove nothing on their own, so it is with artefacts. They must be accompanied by clear witnessed statements showing that they are your work, describing the circumstances under which they were produced, and stating which performance criteria and range statements they claim to meet. For larger artefacts that cannot be treated in this way, you might consider including models in your evidence, but if this is not possible you have only one practical means by which they can be presented in a portfolio and that is photography.

Re-read the section of this chapter about audio-visual evidence (pages 62–66) because all that I have said about photography is relevant in this context. However, the use of photographs or videotapes to record an actual product rather than a fleeting or temporary event is a little more complicated. The best approach is to take a number of different photographs (perhaps of a house or garden restoration, maybe of the installation of a newly fitted kitchen or central heating system) from a variety of angles, or produce a short guided tour on videotape. Then produce a plan of the object and label the photographs to show which view of the plan they represent. Finally, collect together as much witness testimony as you can and support it with other information such as notes, estimates and specifications which may also be relevant. Collate this information with the photographs (or videotape) and plan and include this 'mini portfolio' for each object that you submit as evidence.

Portfolio Guide: Step 35

Before including actual physical products in your portfolio, consider carefully how you will present them, how you will label them and how you will transport them to and from assessment visits.

Consider alternative ways of recording artefacts such as plans, photographs and video tapes.

Are you sure that the artefact is necessary and demonstrates something that cannot be shown in any other way? Do not include it just to be different.

---

9. NVQ STATIONERY

The final category of evidence and one that you must collect for your portfolio is NVQ documentation. Be warned, there can be a mass of this but it is fairly simple to deal with if you follow the suggestions given in this book, particularly those in the following chapter.

Each NVQ is different, each awarding body is different, each assessment centre is different; it therefore follows that there is a huge variety of NVQ paperwork that needs to be dealt with and the names given to the same form may differ between NVQs, awarding bodies and assessment centres. As soon as you enrolled on your NVQ programme you should have developed, with the assessor's help, action plans which specified how to proceed. You should also have been given details of the monitoring or assessment schemes to be used and your assessor may have devised workplace agreements which detailed specific tasks to be undertaken at work. If you have these documents already, keep them safe; if you do not yet have these documents make a note of their titles and discuss them with your assessor.

You will probably find that you have, or will be required to sign several workplace agreements, in fact there is usually one for each unit (or even element) of your NVQ. Whatever happens in your individual case keep all of your workplace agreements. Likewise you may find that you have or you acquire a number of action plans because your needs, demands, skills and accomplishments will change as you progress through your NVQ. Again, keep them all safe; they are vital and will show the assessor and verifier how your professionalism has developed and how your skills have improved during your course or period of assessment. You will collect together a number of documents to do with the monitoring of your progress. This happens because it is not possible to assess your computer skills, for example, in the same way that your verbal communication skills are assessed. Whatever assessment methods are agreed upon with your assessor you must keep copies of them and add them to your portfolio.

You will soon begin collecting observation reports completed by your assessor when they observe you at work; there are likely to be a number of these for the simple reason that your assessor is required to establish your competence over a range of circumstances – the purpose of the range statements in your standards. Keep all observation reports safely and file them in your portfolio with the evidence collected together for the unit to which they relate. Finally, you may be given records of assessment which summarise your competence at different stages of your NVQ programme. Again, keep them safely filed away in your portfolio along with evidence for the unit to which they relate.

Portfolio Guide: Step 36

Keep all NVQ stationery, forms and plans safe – they form an essential part of your portfolio.

CONCLUSIONS

In this and the previous chapter I have discussed every form of evidence that is available for you to collect. Remember, please, that you do not have to collect everything mentioned here, they are a list of possibilities.

Portfolio Guide: Step 37

The examples of evidence in Chapters 6 and 7 are possibilities. You do not need to have all of them in your portfolio but do try to make your portfolio as rich and varied as your work.

Collect those things that are most appropriate for your occupation and which clearly demonstrate how you are competent to claim that you meet specific performance criteria and range statements. I cannot advise you any further on what may or may not be evidence or on how you can present it; what you have to do now is collect evidence and file it in the relevant sections of your portfolio, ie file it with other material for the NVQ unit to which it relates. Some pieces of evidence may relate to several units of your NVQ; if this is the case do not copy the evidence and file it in your portfolio several times. File it only once and with the unit to which it most closely corresponds. You can still use this piece of evidence to claim performance criteria and range statements in other units by indexing the evidence carefully, and indexing is where we go next.

Portfolio Guide: Step 38

Evidence which may be used to meet performance criteria in a number of different NVQ units needs to be included in your portfolio only once. It can be cross-referenced to other relevant units and will still gain you credit for those units.

SUMMARY

Step 31

Decide which examples of graphic information you might use and include them in your portfolio.

Step 32

Decide how you will generate photographic evidence and do it.

Step 33

Label your audiotapes and videotapes clearly and keep copies of them.

Step 34

Label any floppy disks clearly. Produce hard copies of information on the disks. Keep copies of all disks.

Step 35

Clarify how you will present any physical objects and consider alternative ways of presenting them in your portfolio.

Step 36

Keep all NVQ documentation for inclusion in your portfolio.

Step 37

Include as wide a variety of evidence as possible in your portfolio

Step 38

Evidence of performance criteria for a number of units needs to be included in your portfolio only once.

Chapter 8

Organising your evidence

If you have followed all of the advice that I have given in previous chapters, your portfolio should now look quite healthy. However, I expect that one or two vital points have been missed and even those who feel confident might have a niggling doubt at the back of their minds along the lines of 'Have I done this properly?' So this is a good point at which to recap and explain in simple terms what your portfolio should look like.

You should have a large folder or ring binder filled with dividers or plastic wallets. The first divider should separate off from the rest of your material the general introductory paperwork that you should have produced:

- cover
- CV
- organisational profile
- organisational structure
- the overall structure of your NVQ
- copies of existing qualifications.

The other dividers and plastic wallets should be arranged in such a way as to provide a divider and a number of plastic wallets for at least each unit of your NVQ and preferably for each element. At this stage your portfolio will resemble a filing cabinet which has been labelled and filled with suspension files but which is still 90 per cent empty.

As you collect evidence together it should be filed in the relevant 'slot' or plastic wallet in your portfolio along with statements testifying to the authenticity of your work. You should also place in the appropriate plastic wallet any NVQ documentation that has been generated such as Individual Action Plans (IAP), workplace agreements, monitoring schemes, assessment forms and the results of any workplace observations conducted by your assessor. You should also have made arrangements to deal with any audio-visual, computer-generated or photographic evidence which you wish to submit for assessment, and you may even have devised methods to present physical products with your portfolio.

If you have not yet followed these steps now is the time to do so because until you impose some order, sense and structure on your evidence you cannot set it in context or index it ready for final signing off by your assessor. It does not matter how impressive your evidence is, it must be organised, structured and indexed in order to become an acceptable NVQ portfolio that an external verifier will approve as proof of your abilities. If you have not yet organised your collection of evidence, do so now because you cannot follow the rest of this chapter with an evidence collection that is not properly structured.

Portfolio Guide: Step 39

Your NVQ portfolio must be organised if assessors and verifiers are to make sense of it.

The structure you use should be broadly similar to that of your NVQ, ie one section for each element, with the elements grouped together into units.

SETTING YOUR EVIDENCE IN CONTEXT

Evidence collected together to meet the requirements of an element of your NVQ will all be filed together in your folder. The elements which make up an NVQ unit should also be filed together so that everything relating to an individual unit is in one place. This is important because a unit credit is the smallest 'piece' of an NVQ that can be awarded. Check your portfolio now and make sure that evidence for each element is filed together and that elements for the same unit are filed together. Make sure also that there is a divider before and after each 'chunk' of information which refers to a specific NVQ unit.

Each of these 'chunks' of evidence represents your claim to a particular unit of your NVQ and as such each of them has to be 'introduced' to the assessors and verifiers. In other words, each unit has to be set in context and the circumstances under which you produced your evidence have to be explained. You do this by completing a 'unit context sheet', or 'evidence summary sheet', or 'evidence context sheet', or even 'unit summary record' for each unit of your NVQ. There are three reasons for this:

1. The summaries explain how your evidence was produced, in what circumstances and over what time scale.
2. They show that you understand the structure of your NVQ.
3. They usually represent the official signing off point for that unit of your NVQ.

Your unit context sheet (or whatever it is called at your assessment centre) will be completed and signed by you; your assessor will read it, check your evidence and then sign it; an internal verifier will double check your evidence and also sign the sheet. Finally, an external verifier will examine your portfolio and initial or sign the unit context sheet or otherwise record the fact that a unit has been completed and that you should be awarded a credit for that unit.

These sheets also give you an opportunity to draw attention to any evidence which is worthy of special note or which might otherwise be missed. (Perhaps you have evidence which is filed away in a separate container or box file which the verifier does not realise is yours; remember they may be consulting 20 or 30 portfolios at one visit.)

Some awarding bodies issue candidates with pre-printed forms to make the task of setting their evidence in context easier, but many do not, choosing instead to leave the task of record keeping and its management to the assessment centres. You could therefore obtain such forms direct from your assessment centre. If for any reason you have any difficulty in obtaining such documentation, the sample form shown in Figure 8.1 is adequate for your purposes, but you should check with your assessor just in case your awarding body requires you to use a specific form.

If you do not understand any aspect of the procedure of setting your evidence in context you should ask your assessor to explain it to you clearly; in particular your assessor may offer help in

Unit Context Sheet

Unit No. _____ **Title** _____

1. Dates between which the evidence was produced:
   _____ and _____
2. Describe the context in which the evidence was produced. Outline the background to work activities paying particular attention to how underpinning knowledge and understanding was evidenced. (Use additional sheets as required.)

I confirm that all of the performance criteria, the range and the knowledge and understanding have been achieved for this unit of competence.

Name/signature of Candidate: _____ **Date:** _____

Name/signature of Assessor: _____ **Date:** _____

Name/signature of Internal Verifier: _____ **Date:** _____

Figure 8.1 *A unit context sheet based upon those used by the RSA, one of the largest NVQ awarding bodies*

choosing the correct wording when completing the sheets. Remember to use your original sheet as a master copy and make photocopies as you need them. (I would also advise you to work in pencil until you have the correct wording, which can then be transferred to the forms in ink.) Note that ideally the forms should be handwritten in your portfolio and not typed or word-processed because the assessors and verifiers do need to see some samples of your handwriting to satisfy themselves that at its best it is readable and clear.

A simple example of the sort of wording that you might use on the unit context sheets is given below. By completing just a few key phrases that have been left blank (but which are fully explained in the following notes) these paragraphs can be used in, or adapted for, a wide range of NVQs:

'The evidence I have provided for this unit relates to my normal work activities at...
My assessor observed/assessed me at work doing...
on... occasions.
In particular I am including copies of...
which demonstrate my competence in...
My underpinning knowledge and understanding is demonstrated by...'

In the first blank you should include details of your workplace and, if applicable, the branch or location. In the second blank simply state what tasks and under what circumstances your assessor observed or assessed you. In the third space state the number of assessment or observation visits relating to that unit. In the fourth take the opportunity to draw attention to evidence which is of especially good quality and of which you are particularly proud. In the fifth space explain how these particular examples of evidence demonstrate your ability to meet the specific performance criteria of this unit. In the final blank space make every effort to show how your underpinning knowledge and understanding are demonstrated by your evidence.

You can use extra continuation sheets if you wish but do not complicate things unnecessarily; most completed examples that I have seen are perfectly adequate and easily contained on a single form. The forms are best completed as you finish each unit and while the circumstances under which you have worked are still fresh in your mind. Candidates generally find it much more difficult to write out the forms weeks or even months after they originally did the work. Quite apart from this it is very satisfying and encouraging to complete a unit and have it 'signed off' by your assessor leaving you free to concentrate on the next one.

Of those awarding bodies which do not issue pre-printed forms a minority require you to write a short personal statement for each unit or element of your NVQ. This statement serves exactly the same purpose as a unit context sheet: it sets your collection of evidence in context for the verifier and summarises the competencies that your evidence is going to demonstrate. If this applies in your individual case you can still use the wording that I suggested earlier and complete the blank spaces in the manner described here, but do not forget to add the unit and element numbers and titles, and your name.

When you complete unit context sheets or write personal statements to introduce your evidence you will find it a great help to refer to your evidence logbook. In Chapter 4 I urged you to keep a notebook with details of each potential piece of evidence recorded; I also suggested that you should record actions taken by you at the time, the reasons for those actions and the general circumstances under which items of evidence were created. The value of this evidence logbook should be apparent to you and you will find it to be of immense help at this stage of portfolio preparation.

Portfolio Guide: Step 40

Complete a unit context sheet for each unit of your NVQ. Seek the help of your assessor to make sure that you have the correct wording and use the layout suggested here.

If you experience problems when you complete the forms it will more than likely be in the area of demonstrating your underpinning knowledge and understanding. Problems in other areas can easily be dealt with by your assessor and you should not worry about them. I can suggest two ways to help you to deal with the problem of demonstrating underpinning knowledge and understanding. First, you can ask your assessor to set some sort of short test or examination, or even a more extensive project which will give you the 'space' you need to demonstrate your competence. The results of this work or assessment can then be included in your portfolio.

Second, read the underpinning knowledge and understanding requirements for the particular unit you are having difficulty with and obtain any policies and procedures produced by your organisation for those particular circumstances. If such documentation has been produced by your organisation you can then update it, or you can devise an appropriate policy from scratch which clearly demonstrates your grasp of the fundamentals of any particular unit. (Remember to send copies of the suggested new policy or procedure and criticisms of the old one to your manager with a covering memo to generate some extra and hopefully favourable evidence for your portfolio.)

Portfolio Guide: Step 41

Difficulties in demonstrating underpinning knowledge and understanding can be dealt with by:

1. Arranging a short test or longer projects.
2. Writing policies and procedures which clearly illustrate your grasp of the essential issues.

Unit context sheets can be tiresome to complete not least because there will be one of them for each unit of your NVQ. This is why I urged you earlier to write an organisational profile; its purpose was to provide a valuable 'scene-setting' guide for your assessors and verifiers, and it began to force you to think in the broad but directly work-related patterns required by NVQs. Although the sheets are a chore, the notes given here will help you to complete them correctly. There is yet another task to undertake before your portfolio is ready and that is the task of indexing your evidence.

INDEXING EVIDENCE

The unit context sheets serve to provide the background information that describe how your evidence was produced. They set
the scene for your assessors and verifiers, but assessors and
verifiers need more than this: they need to be able to find quickly
the single piece of evidence that demonstrates your ability to meet
performance criteria *a*, *b* or *c* or that shows you working in the
range *x*, *y* or *z*. Therefore your evidence needs to be indexed. I am
sure that you are groaning by now because having just completed
unit context sheets you now have to complete a series of evidence
summary sheets. Perhaps this is an appropriate point at which to
pause and step back from the situation for a moment while we
look at it from another angle.

Your portfolio is an attempt to demonstrate your ability at work;
therefore it needs to be correctly organised and presented. What
will an assessor or verifier think of your ability to organise your
working life efficiently and effectively if you cannot organise your
portfolio of evidence? Indexing your evidence by putting it firmly
in a work-based context and summarising it clearly demonstrates
your organisational ability, your skills at presentation, your deter-
mination to succeed, your attention to detail and your ambition.
So, back to indexing.

Your awarding body may well have supplied you with evidence
summary sheets to make the task of indexing easier. If they have,
then keep the originals safe and work with photocopies; if forms
have not been supplied a sample one is included here. The first
thing that strikes all candidates when they first look at an evidence
summary sheet is how complicated it looks but, if you know what
you are doing, it is really quite simple to deal with.

There are a wide range of evidence summary sheets that might
be used for your NVQ and it wouldn't be possible to give examples
of all of them here. However, all of the forms have a number of
common features and it is straightforward enough to explain their
use by discussing these common features. The evidence summary
sheet links your evidence to the standards and ensures that you
have met all of the performance criteria and range statements. You
will need one evidence summary sheet for each element of each
unit of your NVQ; there is therefore going to be quite a number of
them, usually between 20 and 30, and it is vital that you complete
them correctly.

Portfolio Guide: Step 42

Make photocopies of the evidence summary sheets you have been supplied with. Make one copy for each element of each unit of your NVQ.

A sample evidence summary sheet is shown in Figure 8.2; have a look at it before reading any further.

Completing your name, NVQ title and level, and the unit and element titles and numbers is perfectly simple. The spaces for signatures at the bottom of the sheet are also self-explanatory, but the rest of the form is a little more complicated. Let's take each piece of the form separately and describe its purpose and use.

The first column is headed 'evidence ref' or evidence reference. It may be named differently on the forms that you use, typical names being 'evidence identifier' or 'portfolio reference'. In this column you should write identifying numbers for your items of evidence; each item of evidence should have its own unique number so that it can be quickly and easily found, and so that it is clearly distinguished from other similar pieces of evidence.

The simplest and clearest way to devise these unique numbers is to take the two numbers that represent the element of your NVQ and add consecutive digits to them; this will produce a number such as 8.3.1 which refers to piece of evidence number 1, for element 3, in unit 8. The numbers 8.3.2 and 8.3.3 would refer to pieces of evidence numbers 2 and 3 also for element 3 of unit 8. Exactly the same numbers should be written on your examples of evidence or on small labels stuck to the plastic wallets in which your evidence is filed.

Portfolio Guide: Step 43

Stick labels to the plastic wallets containing your evidence and allocate each item of evidence its own unique number in the manner described here.

The next column is headed 'evidence description' though it may equally well be called 'evidence title', 'source of evidence' or simply

EVIDENCE SUMMARY SHEET

NVQ title: _____ NVQ level: _____

Candidate name: _____

Unit: _____ Element: _____

Performance criteria

Evidence ref	Evidence description	a	b	c	d	e

Range covered

Evidence ref		a	b	c	d	e

Candidate signature: _____ Date: _____

Assessor signature: _____ Date: _____

Figure 8.2 *Evidence summary sheet*

'description'. In this column devise a name or description for your piece of evidence and write it in next to its evidence reference number. Evidence descriptions are intended to be short simple statements such as 'letter to supplier', 'report on customer complaint', 'photographs of display', 'cash handling procedure' and so on.

The remaining five columns are labelled *a* to *e* and are headed 'performance criteria'. In order to complete them you need to read carefully the performance criteria for the element that you are working on. If piece of evidence 8.3.1 described as 'report on customer complaint' appears to you to meet performance criteria *b*, *c* and *e* in your standards you simply place a tick in boxes *b*, *c* and *e*. That is all there is to it. Piece of evidence 8.3.1 is now clearly and acceptably indexed: it is numbered 8.3.1, described as a report on a customer complaint and matches performance criteria *b*, *c* and *e*. You have finished with it and can move on to the next piece of evidence. In this example it will be numbered 8.3.2 perhaps described as a 'complaints procedure' and which you feel meets all of the performance criteria from *a* to *e*; tick all five boxes and move on to the next piece of evidence.

Work though all of the evidence for a particular element in this way. You can photocopy the evidence summary sheets for your NVQ and use as many of them as you need to index a particular element; you are not limited to one sheet.

As you begin to complete evidence summary sheets you may find that you experience some difficulty in working through long documents to find key phrases that demonstrate your claim to meet performance criteria and range statements. Your assessors and verifiers will face exactly the same difficulties as you if you simply present them with a 15-page document and state on your evidence summary sheet that it meets performance criteria 8, in element 2 of unit 7, or whatever. Clearly, this is a sloppy way of working and you run the risk of frustrating your examiners.

You need to find a way of clarifying your evidence and making it apparent which sentence or paragraph supports your claim to meet a particular performance criteria or range statement. You can do this quite easily by annotating your evidence. This means that you draw the assessor's or verifier's attention to the relevant part of a document by highlighting the appropriate section or sections. You can highlight the document by using fluorescent highlighter pens, or by underlining with a coloured pen or by drawing a vertical line at each side of the paragraph. You can also write next to the highlighted area the unit, element and performance criteria, or range statement, numbers which you are claiming. This simple technique can save both you and the assessor a great deal of time and wasted effort.

Annotation of evidence can also take a second form. When you complete evidence summary sheets it may become apparent to you, or to your internal assessor, that it is not completely clear why a particular piece of evidence matches a performance criterion or range statement. If you feel that this is the case with some of your evidence and that it therefore needs some explanation, it is perfectly acceptable to write a short note for the benefit of assessors and verifiers.

This explanatory note should be attached to the document and should be signed. Some notes will be short enough to be written on adhesive 'Post-it' notes and stuck to the document concerned; other explanations might require a lengthier explanation or statement which should be fixed to the outside of the piece of evidence concerned, so that the assessor sees the explanation first and reads your evidence with a clear idea of why the evidence is relevant.

Portfolio Guide: Step 44

Complete your evidence summary sheets for each element of each unit of your NVQ as described here.

Something should immediately be apparent to you: there is going to be a lot of writing and if your collection of evidence is large you are going to generate mountains of additional paperwork. This is one of the reasons that I advised you to complete those optional NVQ units which were closely related to each other; this strategy clearly reduces the amount of evidence that you have to collect because some items can be used two, three or more times. In other words, one piece of evidence can be referred to in a second or third unit and used to meet performance criteria and range statements for those units, as well as for the first unit that they refer to.

To illustrate this we will stick with the same piece of evidence referred to above: 8.3.1 a word-processed report of a customer complaint. It has already been used to meet performance criteria *b*, *c* and *e* of element 8.3, which might be to do with customer care.

Later on in this particular NVQ the candidate might wish to complete a unit about information technology and computing. Finding that she needs examples of word-processed documents to meet the performance criteria of this element and unit, she checks her portfolio and finds a beautiful example of her word-processing skills in piece of evidence 8.3.1. Therefore, on the evidence summary sheet for her information technology element and unit she indexes all of the evidence for this unit and includes on the form details relating to piece of evidence number 8.3.1, checking off which information technology performance criteria it meets. Since item number 8.3.1 is already in her portfolio she needs to do nothing else; she does not have to include a second copy of the document.

Portfolio Guide: Step 45

As you file evidence in your portfolio make a note of any item that you feel might enable you to claim performance criteria and range statements for other elements and units.

When you complete evidence summary sheets for other elements and units include cross-references for your existing evidence thus making maximum use of work that you have already done.

The second half of the evidence summary sheet headed 'range covered' is completed in exactly the same way, except that this time when you complete the tick boxes you are claiming that a piece of evidence meets range statements rather than performance criteria. The forms that you will be presented with in your NVQ will probably be larger than the one shown here and the performance criteria and range statements may be shown next to each other rather than at the top and bottom of the form, but the form will still contain the same basic sections and will work in exactly the manner described here.

Read this section again until you understand it. If you have any problems you must seek the advice of your assessor because these forms are the link between your evidence and the NVQ standards;

without them your portfolio will simply not work. Because these indexing forms are so important the next chapter shows a practical example in detail and repeats much of what has been said here. Read it carefully to see the system in action.

SUMMARY

Step 39

Make sure that your evidence is clearly organised in sections that correspond to the elements and units of your NVQ.

Step 40

Complete a unit context sheet for each unit of your NVQ.

Step 41

Demonstrate underpinning knowledge and understanding by tests, assignments and the production of policies and procedures.

Step 42

Make photocopies of your evidence summary sheets and work in pencil until they are completed correctly.

Step 43

Label and number your items of evidence.

Step 44

Complete evidence summary sheets as described.

Step 45

Make maximum use of your evidence by using it to claim performance criteria and range statements in a number of different elements.

Chapter 9

Practical evidence organisation

The previous chapter looked in some detail at the system used to organise most NVQ portfolios and described how to complete unit context sheets and evidence summary sheets. In this chapter I cover the same ground again but with the aid of a practical example.

The example I have chosen is a level 2 NVQ in the caring professions. Here is a brief version of one of the standards for workers in residential homes: Unit 2 is entitled 'Maintain and control stock, equipment and materials'; it is divided into a number of elements and element 1 is to 'Monitor and maintain stocks of materials and equipment'. Some of the performance criteria for this element are:

(a) supplies and materials are checked and recorded to maintain the required stock levels
(b) stock is rotated to ensure optimum and safe use of resources
(c) any shortfalls in equipment or materials are recorded, reported to the appropriate person and follow up action taken
(d) stock is stored according to manufacturer's recommendations and user requirements
(e) where supply levels fall below the required level the appropriate action is taken and reported to the appropriate person.

And the range statements for the element state the following:

Materials:

(a)   edible and non–edible
(b)   sterile and non–sterile
(c)   hazardous and non–hazardous.

Equipment:

(d)   electrical

(e)   manual.

In order to complete this element, workers in a residential care home need to provide evidence of their day-to-day activities which show them monitoring and maintaining stocks of materials and equipment. Our candidate is a care assistant on the night shift and also has responsibility for supervising the cleaning team and ordering and storing cleaning equipment and materials for them. What sort of evidence might she collect and how should she complete her evidence summary sheets? Figures 9.1–9.4 on pages 89–90 give examples of the evidence she collects for this element.

The evidence looks fairly mundane but does it show the candidate meeting any performance criteria or range statements for the standard given earlier? Look carefully at the standards, read the four pieces of evidence and decide for yourself which performance criteria and range statements are complied with, if any.

Notice that each item of evidence is numbered in the top right-hand corner; the numbers are: 2.1.1, 2.1.2, 2.1.3, 2.1.4, for piece of evidence number 1 for element 1 of unit 2, and pieces of evidence numbers 2, 3 and 4 for the same unit and element. When the candidate completes her evidence summary sheets these numbers are written in the evidence reference column and a brief description of the evidence is given. At this stage the evidence summary sheet looks like the one shown in Figure 9.5 (page 91).

The next stage is to decide which performance criteria and range statements to claim by ticking the relevant boxes.

The first piece of evidence suggests reorganising the store and points out that stock needs reordering. The candidate therefore refers to the standards and claims performance criteria *a*, *d* and *e*, and range statement *a*:

- reorganise the store   performance criteria *a*
- separate food and chemicals   performance criteria *d*
- reorder stock   performance criteria *e*
- edible and non-edible   range statement *a*

The relevant tick boxes are checked off and piece of evidence number 2.1.1 is finished with.

2.1.1

MEMO

To: Catering supervisor   **Date:** 17.1.97

From: A Jackson   **Subject:** Store room

Sorry to ruin your first week here, but the night cleaning shift found several cracked jars of relish in the store. They have leaked on to the lower shelves and some of the packets there have been soaked and damaged.

Do you think it would be a good idea to rearrange stock so that containers of liquids, etc are on the bottom and perishable packs at the top?

I think you should have a look and see what needs replacing.

The mess has been cleaned up but we need to know what happened. Any idea how they got damaged? Perhaps we can claim replacements from our suppliers.

Figure 9.1

2.1.2

MEMO

To: A Jackson   **Date:** 18.1.97

From: Catering supervisor   **Subject:** Store room

Thanks for arranging for the store to be cleaned up after our disaster. You were right, we have lost a few packets of flour and some other stock. I was not aware of how badly the store was organised and I am having everything rearranged along the lines you suggested. I don't know how it happened, but apparently we have had a number of similar problems since we switched to a new supplier. I will keep your informed.

While we are talking about stores, I noticed that the kitchen store contains a carton of six bottles of bleach and I would rather not have them stored with foodstuffs. Do you have a more suitable store anywhere?

I have also asked about a first-aid kit for kitchen staff. I was given your name and told to ask for one officially. Can you help please?

Figure 9.2

2.1.3

MEMO

To: Catering supervisor **Date:** 19.1.97

From: A Jackson **Subject:** Store room

I have ordered a small first-aid kit for the kitchen, one of those fancy ones with blue sticking plasters for catering workers! Will let you know as soon as it arrives. Enclosed is an updated copy of the emergency procedures and a list of first-aiders. Could you display these on the kitchen notice board? They replace all existing procedures.

If you leave the bleach by the store room door I will have it moved tonight. There is a store of cleaning materials and chemicals, in a locked cupboard at the back of the garage.

Figure 9.3

2.1.4

MEMO

To: Manager **Date:** 21.1.97

From: A Jackson **Subject:** Orders

We need to order a number of items as soon as possible and I have made out requisitions for you to sign. They are all standard stuff except for:

1. First-aid kit – we have a new catering manager who is keen to do everything by the book. I suggested the kit on the requisition sheet because it contains blue plasters that should be used by anyone involved in food handling.
2. We need a number of plastic bins for the disposal of hypodermic needles because we now have three residents who are diabetic. I am not sure how many bins we should have, but suggest 12 as a reasonable number.

Figure 9.4

EVIDENCE SUMMARY SHEET

NVQ title: _____ NVQ level: _____

Candidate name: _____

Unit: _____ Element: _____

		Performance criteria				
Evidence ref	Evidence description	a	b	c	d	e
2.1.1	Memo to catering supervisor					
2.1.2	Memo from catering supervisor					
2.1.3	Memo to catering supervisor					
2.1.4	Memo to manager					
		Range covered				
Evidence ref		a	b	c	d	e
2.1.1	Memo to catering supervisor					
2.1.2	Memo from catering supervisor					
2.1.3	Memo to catering supervisor					
2.1.4	Memo to manager					

Candidate signature: _____ Date: _____

Assessor signature: _____ Date: _____

Figure 9.5 *Evidence summary sheet*

The second piece of evidence accepts that the store needs reorganising, asks for chemicals to be moved from the store and asks for a first-aid kit to be provided. As the memo thanks our candidate for suggesting reorganising the store she can use it to support her claim for performance criteria *a*. Asking the candidate to remove chemicals from a food store allows her to make a claim for range statement *a* and asking her to provide a first-aid kit allows her to claim range statement *b*:

- reorganise the store   performance criteria *a*
- remove chemicals   range statement *a*
- supply first-aid kit   range statement *b*

The relevant tick boxes are completed and piece of evidence number 2.1.2 is finished with.

In the third memo our candidate orders a first-aid kit and arranges to separate food and chemicals into different stores allowing her to claim the following:

- supply first-aid kit   range statement *b*
- separate food and chemicals   performance criteria *d* and range statement *a*

She can them move on to the final piece of evidence.

Memo number 2.1.4 orders the first-aid kit and also orders containers for the safe disposal of hazardous waste; the candidate can claim:

- first-aid kit   performance criteria *a*
  range statement *b*
- disposal of hazardous waste   range statement *c*

At this stage the evidence summary sheet will look like Figure 9.6.

A fair number of tick boxes have been completed by careful use of just four pieces of evidence. But this candidate needs more evidence for two reasons. First, all NVQ standards require evidence of your work over a period of time and the evidence presented here covers only one week in January.

EVIDENCE SUMMARY SHEET

NVQ title: _____ NVQ level: _____

Candidate name: _____

Unit: _____ Element: _____

Performance criteria

Evidence ref	Evidence description	a	b	c	d	e
2.1.1	Memo to catering supervisor	✓			✓	✓
2.1.2	Memo from catering supervisor	✓				
2.1.3	Memo to catering supervisor				✓	
2.1.4	Memo to manager	✓				

Range covered

Evidence ref		a	b	c	d	e
2.1.1	Memo to catering supervisor	✓				
2.1.2	Memo from catering supervisor		✓			
2.1.3	Memo to catering supervisor	✓	✓			
2.1.4	Memo to manager		✓	✓		

Candidate signature: _____ Date: _____

Assessor signature: _____ Date: _____

Figure 9.6 *Evidence summary sheet*

Portfolio Guide: Step 46

Make sure that your collection of evidence includes examples that demonstrate your abilities over a period of time. Evidence that is severely restricted in a timeframe will not be approved by your assessor.

The second reason that more evidence is needed is that not all performance criteria and range statements have been claimed. Look again at the completed evidence summary sheet – there are no ticks at all for performance criteria *b* or *c* and performance criterion *e* has been claimed only once. Range statements *d* and *e* have not been claimed and *c* has been claimed only once.

Clearly there are weaknesses in this collection of evidence and this will be pointed out by the assessor. The element cannot be considered to be complete until there are at least two or three claims to have met all performance criteria and range statements.

Portfolio Guide: Step 47

Use your evidence summary sheets as a quick visual check on the development of your evidence collection. If the summary sheets indicate a weakness in your evidence, take action to correct it.

It may be tiresome to complete evidence summary sheets but they have one enormous advantage over other indexing methods: they allow you to see at a glance any weaknesses in your collection of evidence. You can then take steps to rectify the situation and polish your portfolio to perfection. Of course, the whole thing collapses if your evidence is not correctly indexed in the first place.

The other major advantage of this method of indexing is that it is comparatively easy to add extra evidence to your portfolio as the need arises; for example, in order to meet performance criteria or range statements that you were not able to claim first time round. New items of evidence can simply be given identifying numbers and descriptions, they are then entered on the evidence summary sheets and the relevant boxes are ticked. Remember you can use as many evidence summary sheets as you need for each element of your NVQ.

Indexing may be tiresome but it pays handsome dividends if it helps you to bring your portfolio to perfection. Glance through this chapter again and ensure that you understand the process. It might also be helpful to discuss it with other NVQ candidates or with your assessor. As you look at the chapter again, ask yourself: is the evidence well chosen, is it well presented and is it well explained? Good quality evidence has a number of features (discussed in Chapter 4): evidence should be valid, authentic, reliable, sufficient, current, non-confidential and transferable. From these observations we can construct a checklist against which you can judge your evidence.

- Evidence should match as many performance criteria as possible in each unit.
- Evidence should relate to as many range statements as possible in each unit.
- Evidence should demonstrate underpinning knowledge and understanding whenever possible.
- Evidence should demonstrate your personal competence and confidence in your abilities.
- Evidence should speak for itself and require as little explanation from you as possible.

This chapter has another 'hidden' function that you may or may not have spotted. The standards, the evidence and the evidence summary sheets all occur on different pages and in order to follow my narrative or description you will have had to constantly flick backwards and forwards through the chapter. This is exactly what assessors and verifiers do with completed NVQ portfolios.

If the contents are not correctly indexed, the assessors will have difficulty in finding your evidence and its supporting documentation. What they cannot find they cannot award credit for.

SUMMARY

Step 46

Evidence must relate to performance over a reasonable period of time.

Step 47

Use evidence summary sheets to monitor and plan the development of your collection of evidence.

Chapter 10

Other forms of indexing

The method of indexing NVQ portfolios described in Chapter 8 and illustrated in Chapter 9 is the one favoured by many of the larger awarding bodies. Variants of this system are used by many of the smaller awarding bodies to meet the special requirements of their NVQs, but the principles underlying all of the different methods are the same.

The most noticeable difference will relate to the indexing forms used. They are likely to be larger and more complex than the ones shown here because they need enough space to accommodate all of the performance criteria and range statements in each particular element. They will therefore contain many more tick boxes, but they still work in exactly the same way that I have described.

The other major difference may be the practice of printing the forms in landscape (or sideways on), with the longest edge of the page at the top. This practice allows the tick boxes for performance criteria and for range statements to be printed side by side and the evidence description therefore needs to be written on the form only once. The forms used in my examples have performance criteria and range statement tick boxes printed above and below each other and evidence descriptions therefore have to be written out twice. These different arrangements do not alter the basic principle underlying the use of the forms. Whichever way the forms are printed they are used in the same way to link together your collection of evidence and the standard that it is supposed to meet.

Some awarding bodies provide you with a booklet of pre-printed forms; all of the unit context sheets and evidence summary sheets are therefore kept together in one place in a separate port-folio management section of your folder, but the forms are still completed in the manner described here. It is sometimes useful to have your NVQ forms together in a booklet particularly when you come to look at your portfolio to get a general picture of how it is developing and where it may have weaknesses.

It is also handy to have a small guide to your evidence that can be carried around without hauling a hefty ring binder with you. You can produce a small booklet of your forms easily enough by photocopying them and stapling the sheets together. You can then keep these few sheets with you at work and refer to them easily and quickly to see which areas of your NVQ still require the collection or development of evidence.

The booklet idea is also favoured by some assessment centres which also insist on holding on to them at the centre for safe-keeping. (If this applies to you, you can of course ask to make a photocopy of your booklet for your own use.) The reason for assessment centres keeping the booklets of assessment forms is so that the assessors can keep an eye on your progress, plan their assessment visits and advise you on which areas of evidence to concentrate your efforts. Keeping the forms at the assessment centre also has the advantage that you can complete them or update them during your visits to the centre and under the guidance and instruction of your assessor.

SERIAL AND ACTIVITY INDEXING

The method of indexing described in Chapters 8 and 9 is known as 'element indexing' because it indexes your evidence element by element. There are two other methods of indexing, known as 'serial indexing' and 'activity indexing', but they are not as popular as element indexing and your awarding body may stipulate that you use only the element method. Check with your assessor and read your standards carefully to see which indexing methods you may use. Whatever you do, choose an indexing system and stick with that system throughout your portfolio. Do not chop and change from one method to another – if you do your portfolio will cease to mesh together as a sensible, coherent, collection and all of your efforts will have been wasted.

Portfolio Guide: Step 48

Understand the indexing requirements of the awarding body
for your NVQ. Use the method that they advise and apply
the same method throughout your portfolio.

The serial method of indexing is the simplest of all, but it does not
easily allow you to see which performance criteria and range
statements have been met. With serial indexing all of your portfolio
information is kept in one ring binder and all of your evidence in
another. As you collect evidence it is given a simple identifying
number starting at 1 with successive pieces of evidence being given
the next number, 2, 3, 4 and so on. These numbers are listed along
with descriptions of the evidence and are used each time that you
refer to a particular piece of evidence.

The disadvantage of this method of indexing is that you and
your assessor will have to constantly switch from your management folder to your evidence folder to find an individual piece of
evidence. Furthermore, your claim to a particular performance
criteria might refer to pieces of evidence numbers, for example
12, 14, 83 and 91, which means continually flicking through pages
and pages of unrelated evidence. This happens because your
evidence is not structured in any way: it is simply filed in the folder
in the order that it happened to come along. The serial method is
simple precisely because it is unstructured; it is really just a
numerical list of evidence with the assessors being required to put
in the effort of indexing and finding your evidence for themselves.
For this reason I would avoid serial indexing for any but the
simplest and shortest of portfolios.

Activity indexing is, in my opinion, even less suitable for fairly
complex NVQ portfolios and I include it here only for the sake of
completeness. It is best used when the nature of your job lends
itself to collecting and presenting evidence according to particular
activities that could take place at infrequent intervals. For example,
someone completing an NVQ in horticulture might have trouble
demonstrating their ability to harvest cut flowers or tomatoes in
the January frost and snowstorms. Therefore, they might choose
to structure their portfolio around the seasons and the seasonal
activity approach to their work. If they do so, they will be doing

this with the full cooperation and guidance of their assessor – do not attempt this yourself unless it is a realistic option that has been decided on after careful discussion with your assessor.

OTHER ASPECTS OF INDEXING

When you completed your evidence summary sheets you will have had probably the first real opportunity to study your evidence carefully and it is possible that you have noticed a number of things that need explaining to assessors and verifiers. I am thinking particularly of abbreviations, jargon and people's names, titles and job roles. It is good practice to explain anything in your evidence that does not stand alone and explain itself. If an assessor or verifier does not understand something in your evidence, they cannot reasonably be expected to award credit for it. Do not allow this to happen to you.

If you have used a number of abbreviations take the time to produce a list of them and explain each one in turn (just as I have done in this book). Arrange them in alphabetical order, spell out the words in full and if necessary give an explanation of the phrase.

Portfolio Guide: Step 49

If your evidence uses large numbers of abbreviations prepare an alphabetical list of them along with the name or phrase in full and a brief explanation of its meaning or significance.

You should also take the time to do exactly the same thing with any jargon or technical phrases, and particularly with any language that is specific to your workplace and the organisation for which you work. The most common source of confusion is referring to documents or forms by the names that you use at work each day, but which are totally meaningless to an outsider. In order to get round the problem you need to produce a glossary, or dictionary, or list of such phrases with an explanation of their meanings. A glossary is included in this book and you can see that it follows a simple alphabetical layout and gives a brief, clear explanation of each word that is listed.

Portfolio Guide: Step 50

If your evidence uses large numbers of technical phrases or phrases that are peculiar to your organisation then you need to include a glossary to explain them clearly to your assessors and verifiers.

If your portfolio includes numbers of foreign words and phrases (and especially if you include whole pieces of evidence in other languages), do not assume that assessors and verifiers will understand them. With words and phrases it is wise to include them in your glossary or to develop a separate glossary for them alone. Obviously any evidence that is in a foreign language needs special treatment, particularly if the actual contents of the document allow you to claim specific performance criteria or range statements.

With simpler documents it will be enough to provide a straightforward explanation of their significance. For example, if you have a number of 'thank you' notes from customers and one of them is in French, a simple explanation that this letter is a letter of thanks from a French customer will be adequate. However, if the document is a detailed explanation, plan or discussion and allows you to claim a specific performance criterion or range statement, you will need to provide a clear description of the document or even a full translation and an explanation of its significance and the circumstances under which it came to be included in your evidence. If you cannot do this, clearly it has no place in your portfolio of evidence, which is intended to be a demonstration of what you know, what you can do and what you understand.

Portfolio Guide: Step 51

Foreign words and phrases need to be explained and, if there are large numbers of them, included in a separate glossary. Whole items of evidence in foreign languages need a clear explanation in English and could require a full English translation.

The final group of terms used in your evidence that might need clarification are people's names, their job titles and roles. If you produced an organisational structure as described in Chapter 5 you might not need to do anything further. But if your evidence refers to people whose roles and functions are not clear, you might find it useful to list them in alphabetical order and explain their relevance to your evidence. In particular, it can be useful to list anyone who has acted as a witness for you or who has signed documentation on your behalf. In the latter case, you might also consider including a sample list of signatures or initials as this will help your assessor and verifier to establish the authenticity of your evidence.

Portfolio Guide: Step 52

If your collection of evidence refers to a number of people whose roles, job titles and relationship to you is unclear, you will need to prepare a simple 'cast of characters' to clarify matters for your assessors and verifiers.

The only pitfalls of evidence to which you might need to give more thought are any special symbols or logos that might be used in your occupation. For example, electricians use symbols on circuit diagrams, landscape gardeners use them on plans, proofreaders use them to mark up documents and so on.

Symbols are mostly used in drawings and maps and are best explained on the sheets where they occur. However, if you use any 'shorthand' of this nature, do not assume that assessors and verifiers will be familiar with it. Take the time to provide a simple 'key', like the ones on maps which list the symbols and explain in simple terms the significance of each one.

Portfolio Guide: Step 53

Special symbols, logos, trademarks, characters and other forms of visual shorthand need clarification if there is any doubt about assessors and verifiers being familiar with them. If this applies in your case, you need to prepare a 'key' to explain the use and meaning of such symbols and characters.

CONTENTS PAGE

The final step in indexing your portfolio will be to produce a contents page. This describes the layout of your folder and gives it that well-organised, professional final touch. The contents page should be on not more than a single sheet of A4 paper and should be the first page in your folder after the cover sheet. It does not need to be particularly complex, a simple description is sufficient.

Head the sheet 'Contents' and then list the main sections of your portfolio in the order that they will be found in your folder. You might find it useful to divide the contents into four main sections: introduction, background, management, evidence. The contents of each section can then be listed giving a completed sheet like the following.

Contents

Introduction:	abbreviations
	glossary
	people involved
Background:	CV
	job description
	job/performance reviews
	organisational profile
	organisational structure
	existing qualifications
Management:	overview of NVQ standards
	action plans
	NVQ monitoring information
Evidence:	subdivided into units and elements
	unit context sheets
	evidence summary sheets

Portfolio Guide: Step 54

Produce a contents page for your portfolio and file it at the front of your folder.

Having filed your contents page your portfolio is now complete. All that remains is to let your assessor know, wait for the verifier's visit and collect your certificate.

Portfolio Guide: Step 55

Inform your assessor that you have finished.

Of course, having expended so much effort on your portfolio you do not want to leave it sitting on a shelf gathering dust. It can be used in other ways to advance your career and qualifications and the next chapter looks at some of these bonuses.

SUMMARY

Step 48

Select the appropriate portfolio indexing method and use it throughout your portfolio.

Step 49

Produce a list of abbreviations.

Step 50

Produce a glossary.

Step 51

If you have used foreign words or phrases ensure that they are explained in a glossary.

Step 52

Prepare a list of people referred to in your portfolio and explain their roles.

Step 53

Explain any special symbols and characters used in your evidence.

Step 54

Produce a contents page.

Step 55

Tell your assessor that you have finished.

Chapter 11

Using your portfolio

Having successfully completed your portfolio, you will find that it is carefully checked by your assessor and a date will be fixed for an internal verifier to double-check that everything is satisfactory. Your portfolio will then be left at the assessment centre until an external verifier's visit can be arranged. This visit is the final step in gaining your NVQ and if everything goes without a hitch, your portfolio will be returned to you followed, some time later, by your NVQ certificate.

Having done so much work to gain your NVQ it seems a shame to leave your portfolio on a shelf or forgotten at the back of a cupboard, because it can still be of benefit to you. The first and most obvious use for your portfolio is to assist you in your progression through NVQ levels. Much of the material that you have already prepared can be re-used, for example: your CV (duly updated to include your NVQ), your job descriptions and performance appraisals, your organisational profile and structure. With a new cover and an overview of your new NVQ standards, the introductory section of a new portfolio is already completed.

In moving through NVQ levels you have a tremendous advantage compared with your situation when you began your first NVQ programme; you have already been through the NVQ process and you are experienced in preparing a successful NVQ portfolio. This experience will give you a flying start on any new NVQ that you decide to undertake either at a higher level or in an entirely new subject area.

As I mentioned at the start of this book, portfolios are commonly used by people in creative occupations to show examples of their most accomplished work and they are frequently used by tradesmen and self-employed workers as a means of providing examples of their work which would otherwise not be seen by prospective customers. Now that you have a stock of evidence about your work there is nothing to stop you from developing a similar portfolio to display your best work and your greatest achievements.

This approach can be of benefit in a surprisingly wide variety of occupations: gardeners, hairdressers, car restorers, upholsterers, craft potters and many others can recycle their photographic evidence and other examples of their work in this way. It is easy enough to see how 'products' made by people in these categories can be displayed to prospective clients, but the story does not end there. There is absolutely no reason why people in clerical occupations, and in any occupation at all, cannot recycle the best of their work from their NVQ portfolio and use it to sell themselves to prospective employers and customers.

If you are stuck for ideas of what to include in a portfolio of this sort, refer to Chapters 6 and 7 about collecting evidence, to refresh your memory. Examples of well-produced word-processing, advertisements, maps and plans, conference itineraries, balance sheets, reports that you have written, guides that you have produced... the list is endless. Select the best of them and, using the skills of portfolio preparation that you have developed on your NVQ programme, group them together under headings appropriate to your occupation. File them in a smart new ring binder along with your CV, copies of your qualifications and details of any staff development or work-based training that you have completed.

This personal portfolio can then accompany you to job interviews, it can be shown to prospective employers to reinforce your answers to their questions, and it can be used to support applications to join a course of study at college or university. More and more employers and organisations are willing to accept personal portfolios like this as evidence of the strengths and skills that people have developed through experience.

A personal portfolio is also a handy place to keep a copy of the letter and application form that you submitted, and a list of the questions that you would like to ask at interview and which you might otherwise forget in the heat of the moment. It is professional to have a portfolio of this sort and it is also a useful psychological prop which can help you out in situations where you might have forgotten the answer to a vital question or cannot remember your response to one of the questions on the application form. Everything that you need will be at your fingertips.

A professional portfolio is vital when it comes to filling in application forms – no more hunting through drawers and shoeboxes full of papers to find your certificates or the name and address of an employer that your worked for ten years ago. Everything will have been prepared in advance and is ready for you to copy out.

It might sound as though I am suggesting developing a personal portfolio as a 'dumping ground' for all the odds and ends that you don't know where to keep, but this is not the case. A good personal portfolio is a useful tool that will help you to progress and achieve your aims. It is a formative and not a summative document; in other words, it is not only a statement of the 'sum' of what you are at the moment but it is a tool to help you to 'form' what you want to be in the future.

As you have worked through this book and prepared your NVQ portfolio you have been through a formative process, one that changed your attitude to your work and helped you to become a more capable, efficient and professional worker. A personal portfolio helps you to continue that process. It is a flexible career management tool. It is flexible because you can change it and add to it as you gain in experience and develop new strengths and skills. You can also use it flexibly by taking parts from it as needed or presenting the whole collection depending upon the circumstances.

It is worth making the effort to develop this tool using the techniques learned on your NVQ programme because it can help you to manage your career more effectively, take control of your training and development, and monitor your professional and career development.

A personal portfolio can also be a means of recording your achievements so that you can identify, celebrate and build upon your own strengths. You can use it to help you to see which skills you still want to develop and to plan what you want to do next. This is important because in today's world of work we all need to continually update and upgrade our skills as our needs and circumstances, and those of our employers change.

Organisations have changed dramatically in the last 20 years and they now want employees who:

- have a broad overview of their work
- are able to change roles

- are keen to learn new skills
- are able to cope with change
- are committed
- can work in teams
- are adaptable and flexible
- are customer or client focused
- and are profit and efficiency focused.

All these qualities can be clearly illustrated in a good well-presented professional or personal portfolio. Simply collecting evidence about your work, just as you did with your NVQ, will continually highlight how you can achieve the characteristics required by employers. Your evidence will show you how you can become more responsive to change, how you can become more confident and motivated, how to become more self-assured and clarify what job role will suit you best.

Too many people are passive when it comes to career management: they sit back and wait for things to happen or opportunities to present themselves. Producing a portfolio makes you active and forces you to take responsibility for your career.

The professional portfolio is an enabling framework. Just as the NVQ portfolio that it grew out of enabled you to obtain a new or additional qualification, so the professional portfolio can open new avenues for you.

Chapter 12

Candidates with communication difficulties

Throughout this book, and particularly when I have discussed evidence, I have assumed that all NVQ candidates are able to see and hear perfectly well and are capable of reading and writing with ease, but of course this is not always the case. NVQ candidates who have a visual or hearing impairment and candidates who have dyslexia might face special problems when they attempt to collect evidence and display it in a portfolio. But these problems are not insurmountable; anyone who is already doing a particular job simply needs to prove that they are doing it satisfactorily in order to gain their NVQ certificate. There is no reason at all why candidates with communication difficulties cannot offer this proof and gain their NVQs.

Candidates with any degree of hearing impairment may have particular difficulties in understanding spoken instructions, in making verbal responses to questions and, if they have difficulties learning written language, may also experience problems in producing good quality written evidence. If this applies to you, you must be absolutely certain that not only your employer but also your NVQ assessor are aware of your situation. This is vital for two reasons.

First, the assessor can take action to ensure that you are not unfairly penalised at any stage of the NVQ process because of your difficulties. Indeed, the NCVQ will not accredit any awarding body that does not take reasonable steps to ensure that candidates are not excluded from the qualification on grounds of age, sex, race, culture or physical ability. Having said that, it is sometimes not possible to relax or interpret NVQ standards in such a way as to get round the problem. If a standard requires candidates to use the telephone it is easy enough to accomplish this by using a minicom, but if a motor vehicle candidate is required to tune an engine by listening to its pitch things are not quite so straight-forward.

Second, assessment centres are usually colleges of further education and have the ability to obtain funding that will enable them to supply specialist equipment and support workers to assist students and NVQ candidates to complete their chosen pro-gramme. In your case this might mean the availability of a trained communicator to sign between you and assessors or verifiers during assessment visits. I cannot do more than urge you to find out what support is available and to take advantage of it.

Candidates who are blind or visually impaired also have special problems that need to be resolved. If you are in this situation you can still produce good quality written evidence using whatever means you normally use to produce written communications. It is perfectly acceptable to submit documents in your portfolio which are in large print and on A3 paper if that is how you normally communicate; it is also acceptable to submit documents produced with any word-processing and speech synthesis system that you are in the habit of using.

Raised character languages such as Braille and Moon, and embossed or raised character diagrams, maps and plans may also be used. Of course, this will completely baffle your assessors and verifiers – you must give them plenty of advance warning and supply copies in plain English. If you do not then the relevant evidence will be left unassessed until such time as they can have it interpreted (not all assessment centres have Braille specialists readily available).

You also need to make sure that your assessment centre is aware of your situation and the extent of your visual impairment because, as I have already said, they may well have specialised equipment and support workers on hand to make your task that much easier. The further education college that I work for makes available to students with visual and hearing impairments all of the following:

- still and video cameras for loan
- portable tape-recorders for loan
- electronic speaking dictionaries for loan
- electronic notebooks for loan

- combined word-processing and speech synthesis computers
- text enlargers
- flat-bed scanners
- closed circuit television
- translation of written documents to and from Braille
- trained support workers who can read and write for you
- trained sign language communicators.

This represents a rich resource for candidates who might otherwise struggle with the problems of producing and presenting evidence, and these resources are duplicated at other further education centres. You must find out what support your assessment centre can offer you – and remember that the centre wants you to complete your qualification successfully because it enhances its reputation.

The more unusual or non-standard forms of evidence that I have described in earlier chapters can all be readily used by candidates with visual and hearing difficulties. You should therefore explore fully the options provided by audiotapes, videotapes and photography, which can make your tasks of producing and presenting evidence a little easier by reducing the necessity to produce much hard-won written evidence. You should also develop the habit of using observation visits, short tests, witnessed statements and even simulations to meet performance criteria and range statements where it is particularly difficult for you to generate evidence; these assessment methods can do away with the need for some evidence requirements. This, of course, is another powerful reason for enlisting the aid of your assessor.

I have specifically drawn attention to hearing and visual impairment because it is by writing, organising, hearing and seeing that evidence is more often presented, and these means of communication are at the heart of the NVQ process. I have not addressed physical disability because open communication is not impaired, and those people already active in an occupation should be able to collect evidence about their work and present it in a portfolio. Nonetheless, you should find out about the extent of support that assessment centres are able to offer and seek whatever support you need.

Candidates who have dyslexia could also face problems when trying to collect, present and index evidence of their abilities at work, particularly if they have what is known as 'organisational dyslexia'. They must enlist the help of their assessor and should make full use of the possible range of evidence that I have described since much of it need not be written. Where dyslexic candidates do produce written evidence it is perfectly acceptable to word-process the work making full use of the spelling and grammar facilities available on the machines. They must also ensure that their assessors and verifiers are aware of their particular needs and they should be ready to provide proof of the extent and exact nature of their dyslexia.

The proof required will be the results of an official dyslexia assessment or the results of an assessment made by an educational psychologist. If a candidate has problems in obtaining this proof their NVQ assessment centre (particularly if it is a college of further education) will almost certainly be able to arrange the required assessment and will be able to guide and reassure the candidate during this process.

Although it may be tiresome, it is important to obtain this official documentation because your assessor will then be able to offer extra help and guidance. The exact nature of this help will differ between awarding bodies, and from one NVQ to another because of the different demands made on workers in different occupations. The best advice that I can give is to ask. Find out what is available and use it.

Finally, no awarding body is allowed to exclude a candidate on any grounds other than their ability to do the job. If you feel that you are not being treated fairly you have the right to complain, not only to your awarding body but also to the NCVQ, which takes such complaints very seriously indeed.

Chapter 13

Further information

I do not wish to burden you with a lot of additional reading, so this chapter is quite short and refers to only five other books and to two organisations that you can approach for help. (Full details of the books and addresses of the organisations are given on pages 115–16.)

To find out more about qualifications in general, the annual publication from the Careers and Occupational Information Centre (COIC) called *Occupations* contains a short two-page description of the structure of qualifications in this country. The rest of the book contains information on approximately 600 jobs, including pay, conditions, qualifications and training. This gives you a rough idea of which NVQs might be available in which occupational areas. You should be able to consult the book in the reference section of your local library, in the careers section of a college library, or you can contact COIC direct for information.

A useful book about the whole area of vocational qualifications, which also describes the differences between NVQs and GNVQs, is *Getting into Vocational Qualifications* by Katherine Lea. If you would like to read more about the philosophy of NVQs in particular, you cannot do better than read *NVQs and How to Get Them* by Hazel Dakers.

If you need to find out more about a specific NVQ or the availability of NVQs in your area of work, contact the NCVQ direct or visit the local library and consult the reference book *Directory of Vocational and Further Education*. This contains two very useful sections:

1. An alphabetical list of Lead Bodies along with their occupational areas, addresses and telephone numbers. Each of the

Lead Bodies can be contacted direct for further information and advice.
2.   A list of awarding bodies along with their occupational areas, addresses, telephone numbers and named contacts. Again, the awarding bodies may be contacted for more information including details of assessment centres in your area. The largest awarding bodies for NVQs are BTEC, CGLI, RSA and SCOTVEC (addresses are given on page 116).

The NCVQ has produced a database of all NVQs and you should be able to consult this in most large libraries. The database does not require computer skills in order to operate it successfully, and it can quickly help you to pinpoint a specific NVQ, along with the addresses and telephone numbers of all awarding bodies offering that particular NVQ.

If you have any difficulties in finding a Lead Body for your occupational area, you will be able to obtain assistance from the National Council of Industry Training Organisations (NCITO), while your local Training and Enterprise Council (TEC) will be able to offer more general advice about the NVQs available in your area. (You can trace your local TEC in the telephone directory or seek help from the TEC National Council.)

Finally, if you have completed an NVQ at level 3 and would like to progress to a higher level, there is an excellent guide to more complex portfolios, time-management and career development by Greg Whitear, *NVQ and GNVQ Handbook and Guide to Career Success*.

BIBLIOGRAPHY

Careers and Occupational Information Centre (1996) *Occupations*, COIC, Bristol.

Dakers, Hazel (1996) *NVQs and How to Get Them*, Kogan Page, London.

Lea, Katherine (1995) *Getting into Vocational Qualifications*, Trotman, London.

Pitman (1997) *Directory of Vocational and Further Education*, Pitman, London.

Whitear, Greg (1995) *NVQ and GNVQ Handbook and Guide to Career Success*, Pitman, London.

ADDRESSES

General

Careers and Occupational
Information Centre (COIC)
PO Box 348
Bristol, BS99 7FE
Tel: 0117 977 7199

National Council for
Vocational Qualifications
(NCVQ)
222 Euston Road
London, NW1 2BZ
Tel: 0171 387 9898

National Council of Industry
Training Organisations
(NCITO)
10 Amos Road
Unit 10
Meadowcourt
Sheffield, S9 1BX
Tel: 01742 619926

Training and Enterprise
National Council
Westminster Tower
3 Albert Embankment
London, SE1 7SX
Tel: 0171 735 0010

Awarding bodies

Business and Technology
Education Council (BTEC)
Central House
Upper Woburn Place
London, WC1H 0HH
Tel: 0171 413 8400

City and Guilds of London
Institute (CGLI)
46 Britannia Street
London, WC1X 9RG
Tel: 0171 278 9460

Royal Society of Arts
Examinations Board (RSA)
Progress House
Westwood Way
Coventry, CV4 8HS
Tel: 01203 470033

Scottish Vocational Education
Council (SCOTVEC)
Hanover House
24 Douglas Street
Glasgow, G2 7NQ
Tel: 0141 248 7900

Glossary

Accreditation of Prior Learning: the assessment and accreditation of existing learning, knowledge, skills and achievements.

Accredited: licensed or approved to award NVQ certificates.

Action Plan: a plan of action that you need to take in order to generate evidence to meet NVQ standards.

Assessment Centre: an organisation through which NVQ assessment is carried out.

Assessor: someone who judges your performance against the national NVQ standards and guides you through an NVQ programme.

Awarding Body: an organisation approved to provide NVQ programmes and make the award of NVQ certificates.

Candidate: someone working on an NVQ programme, the equivalent of a student in a college or university.

Competence: proven ability to meet the national standards for your work.

Criteria: standards or conditions against which your actions are judged and found to be competent or not.

Element: the smallest part of an NVQ unit; when an element is finished it has to be collected with other elements in order to complete the unit.

Evidence: information or proof that the national standard for your job has been met by your performance.

Evidence Indicator: statements in some NVQ standards describing the type and quantity of evidence which candidates must present in their portfolios.

Individual Action Plan: an action plan tailored to your individual, personal needs.

Lead Body: the organisation responsible for defining the national standards of performance for your occupational area.

Level: grade. NVQs are awarded at five levels, 1 being the lowest and 5 the highest.

Mandatory: compulsory. Some NVQ units for each occupation must be completed; they are said to be mandatory.

Monitoring: checking what is happening. In your case, this means checking your progress on your NVQ programme.

Optional: a unit that you might choose to complete if you wish. All NVQ candidates have a choice of optional units that they complete as well as their mandatory units.

Performance Criteria: a statement of the performance necessary for you to reach the national standard for your job. Performance criteria explain what has to be done or covered.

Portfolio: a collection of evidence presented for assessment to establish your competence at your job.

Programme: an NVQ scheme of work roughly equivalent to a course of study at a college.

Range Statement: a statement that specifies the different circumstances under which you must demonstrate your competence.

Standards: the basis for assessment of your evidence and performance. Standards explain what has to be tested or assessed, not what you need to study.

Underpinning Knowledge and Understanding: the basic or fundamental things that you must know and be able to explain in order to do your job to meet the requirements of the NVQ standards.

Unit: the smallest part of an NVQ that can be assessed and for which a certificate can be awarded. Units are made up of elements.

Validated: approved. An assessment centre is said to be validated if it has been checked by an awarding body and found to be fit to offer a particular qualification.

Verifier: someone who monitors assessment procedures and ensures that they meet the national standards.

Abbreviations

APL	Accreditation of Prior Learning
BTEC	Business and Technology Education Council
CGLI	City and Guilds of London Institute
CV	curriculum vitae
GNVQ	General National Vocational Qualification
IAP	Individual Action Plan
NCITO	National Council of Industry Training Organisations
NCVQ	National Council for Vocational Qualifications
NVQ	National Vocational Qualification
RSA	Royal Society of Arts Examinations Board
SCOTVEC	Scottish Vocational Education Council
SVQ	Scottish Vocational Qualification
TEC	Training and Enterprise Council

Index